Snap, Crackle, and Pep

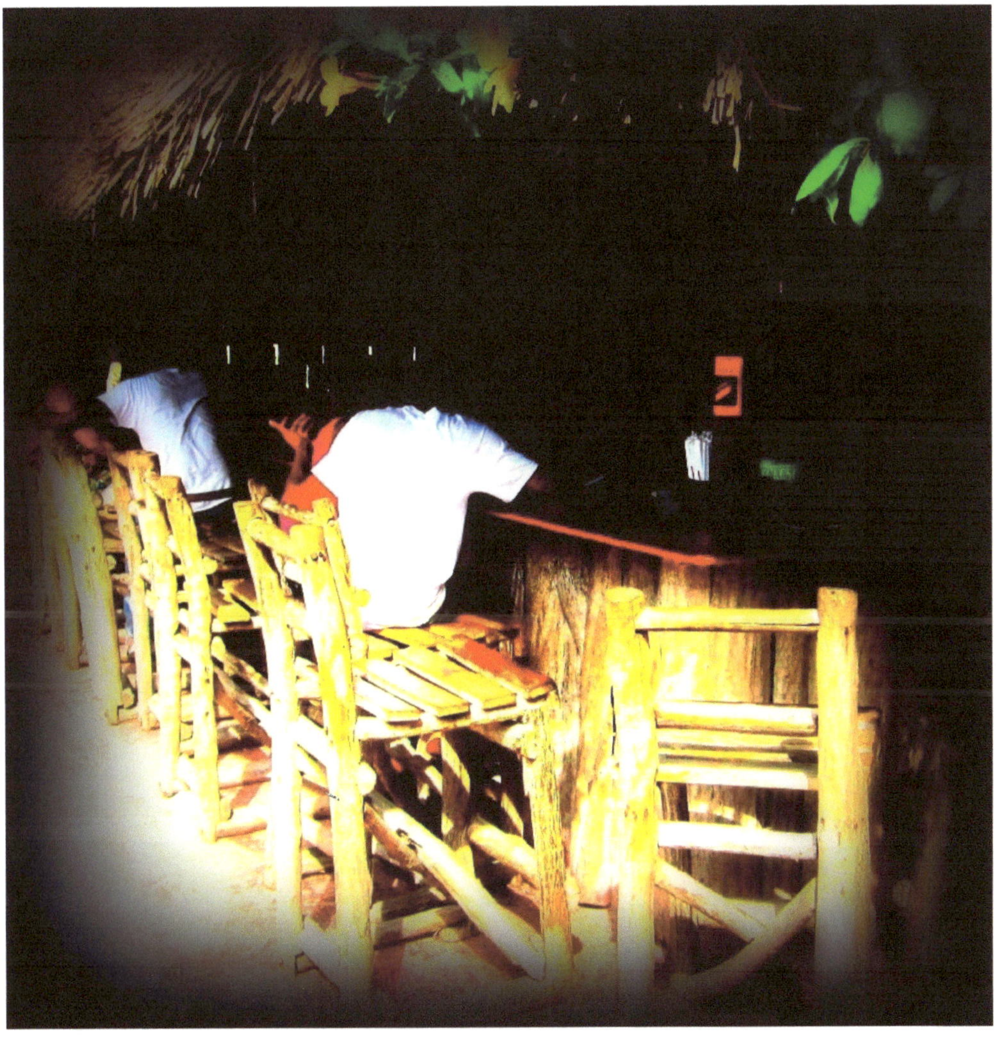

Keith Pepperell

Copyright © 2017 Keith Pepperell

All rights reserved.

ISBN-13: 978-1974259694

ISBN-10: 1974259692

DEDICATION

To my spawn Jack, Lydia, and Alex all of whom take some jolly good snaps. And to the late great Trevor Lang, Stephen Knapper, and Joey Waldon.

ACKNOWLEDGMENTS

To all those poor buggers, objects, animals, and vistas that have unwillingly stood still or moved slightly to the left while I fumbled around and attempted to get them almost in the frame.

THE IMAGES

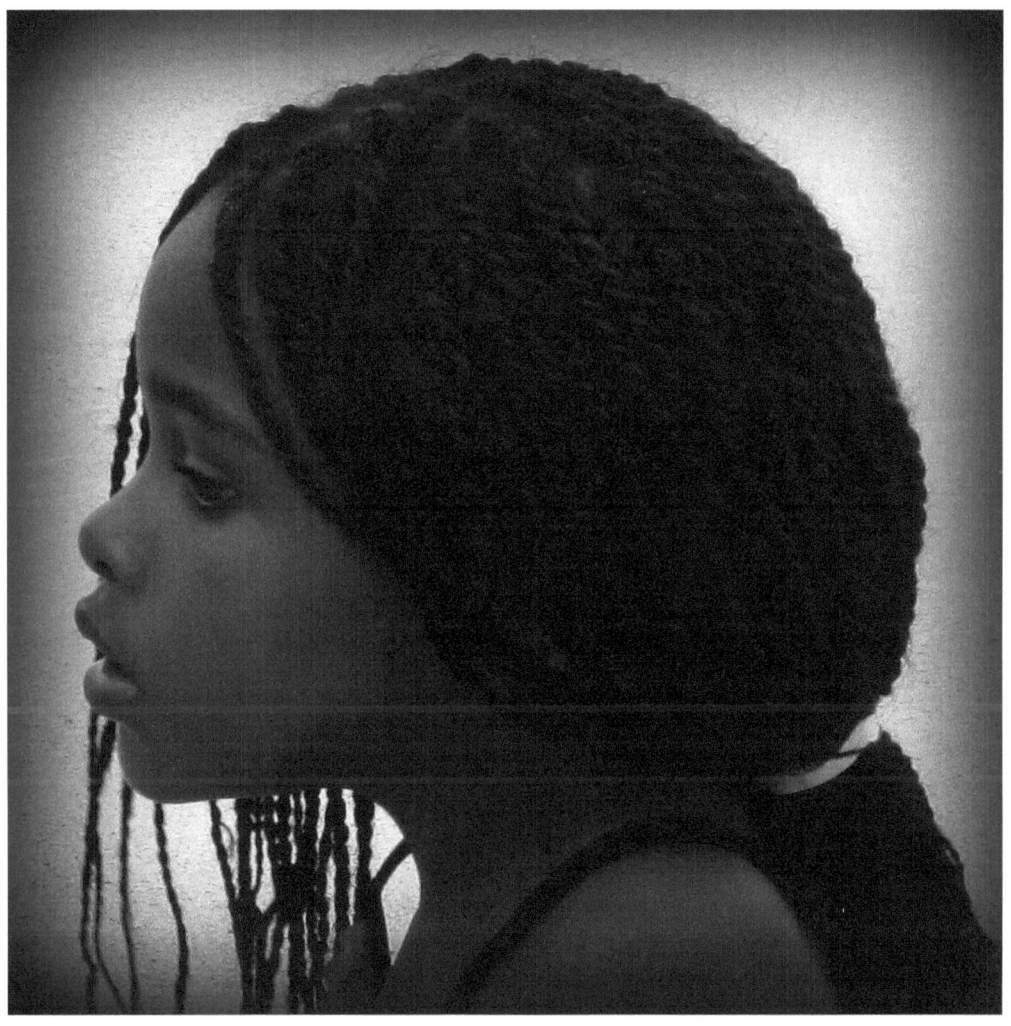

1. A Young Lady on a Beach in Mexico

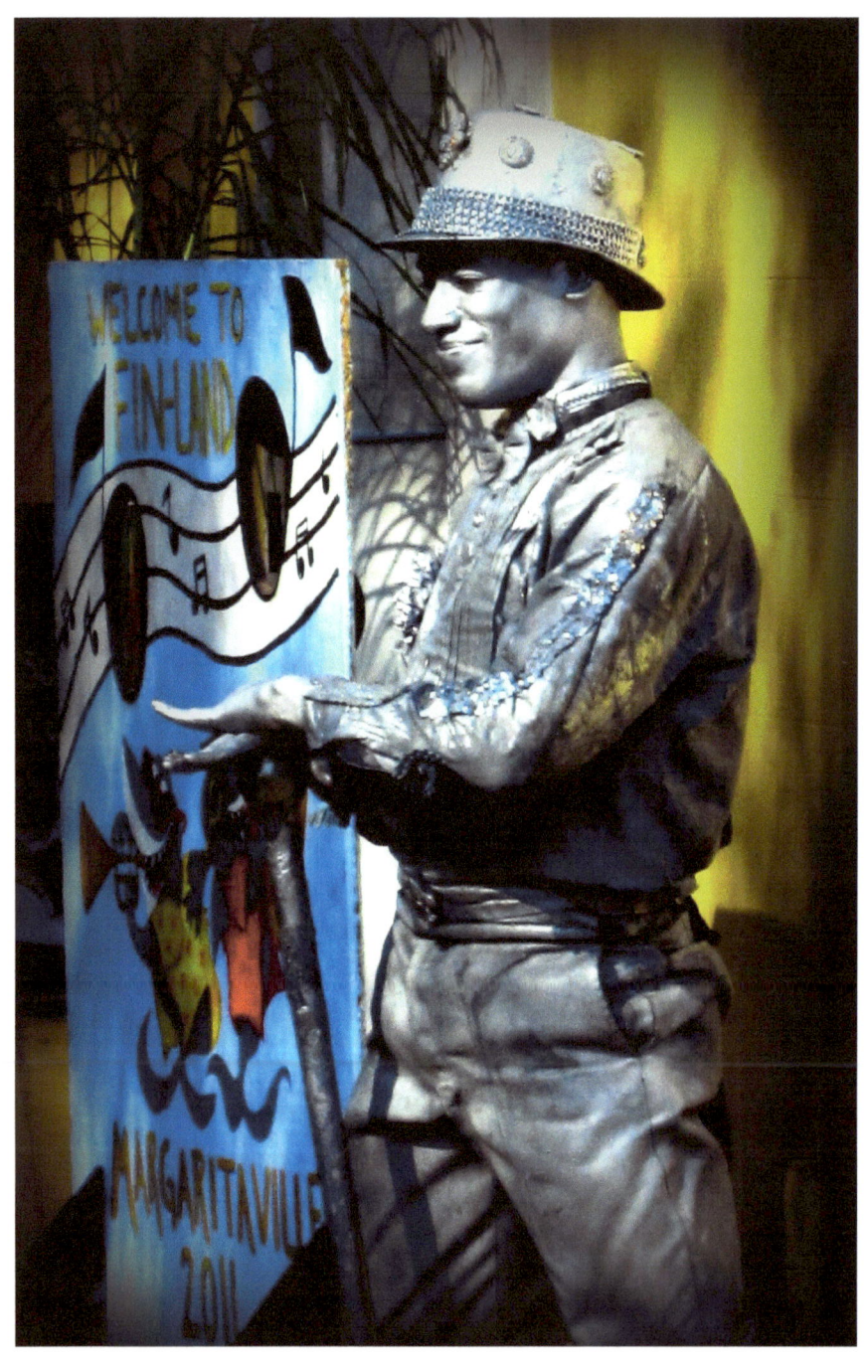

2. Street Performer – New Orleans

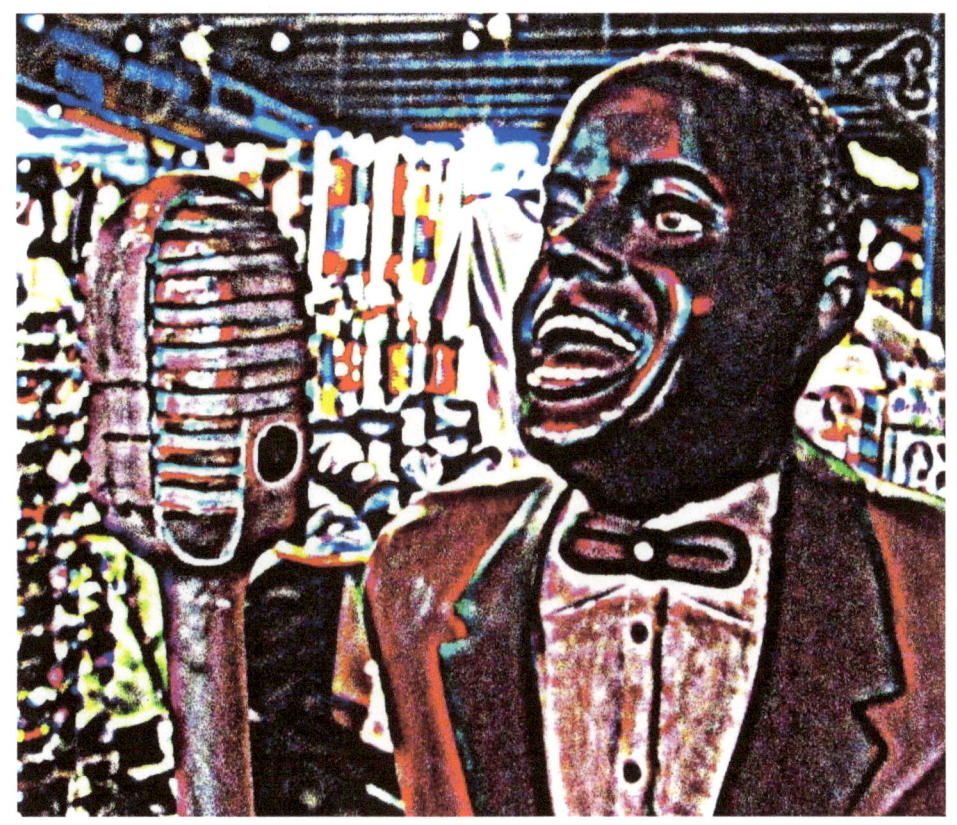

3. House of Blues – New Orleans

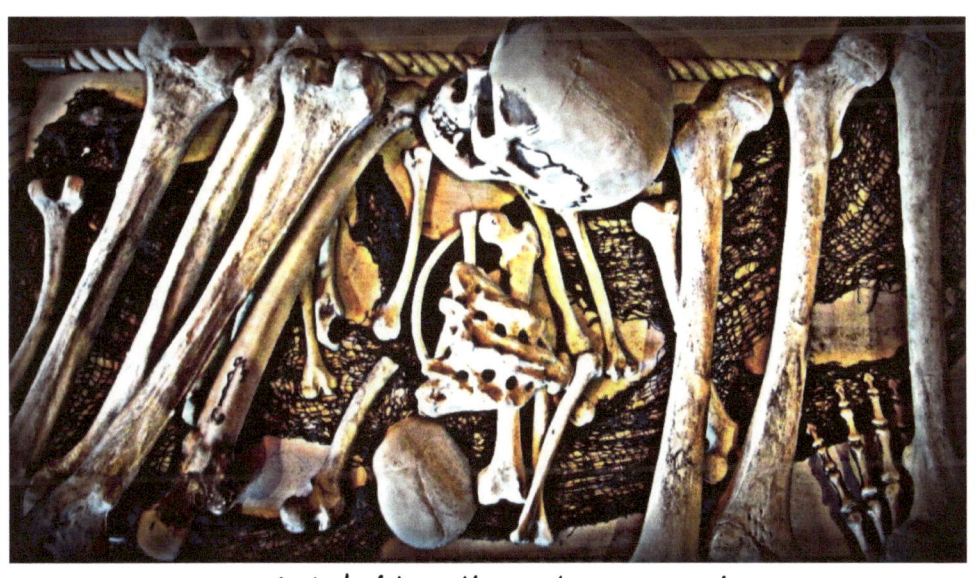

4. Waiter there's a ………!

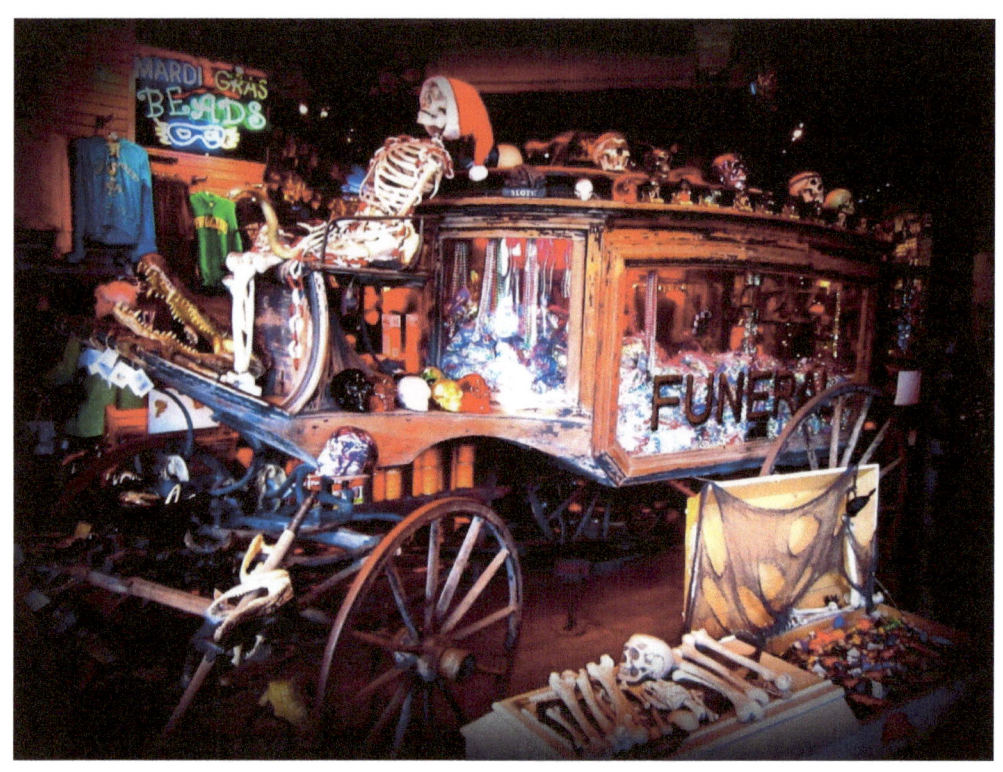

5. Uber Goest Thou?

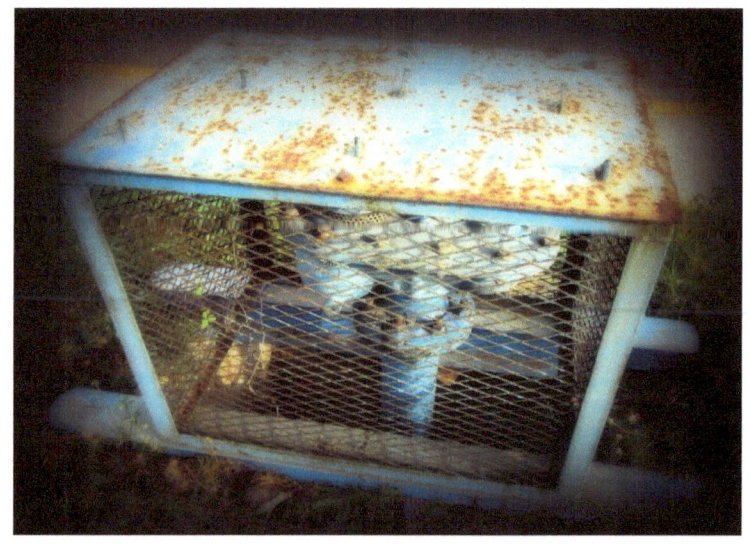

6. Sorry, I'm a Bit Rusty

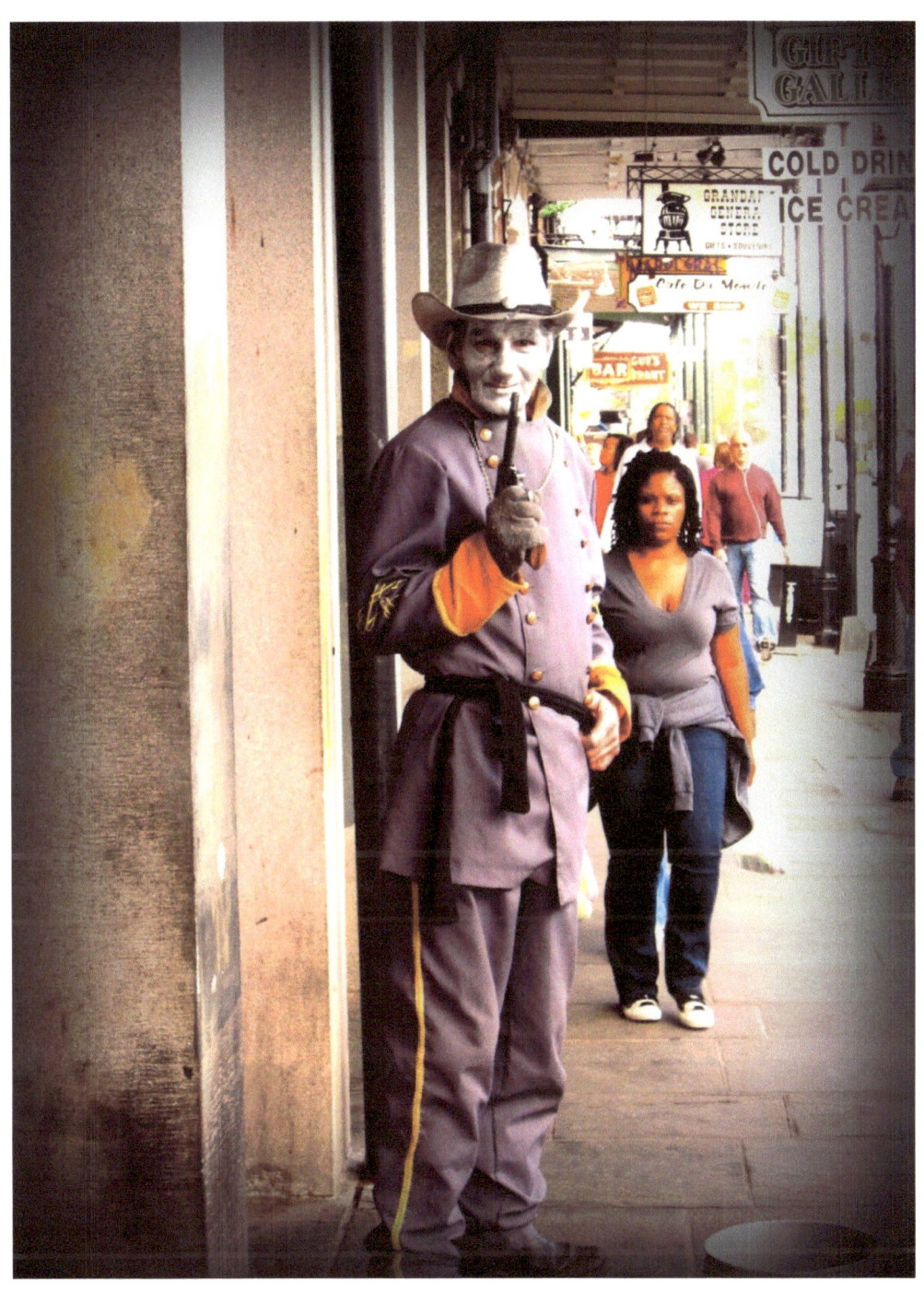

7. Be Civil!

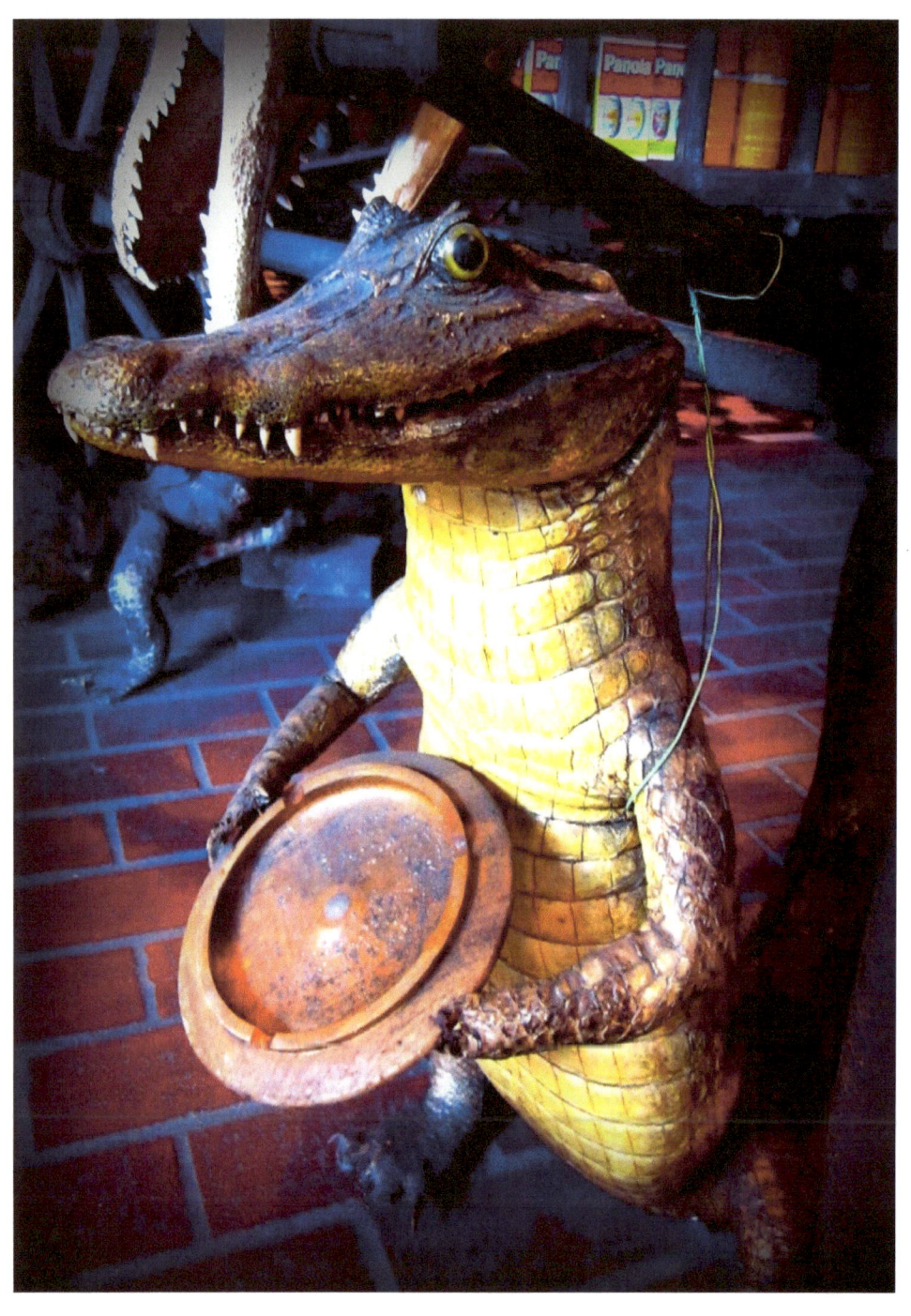

8. You'd Better Make it Snappy

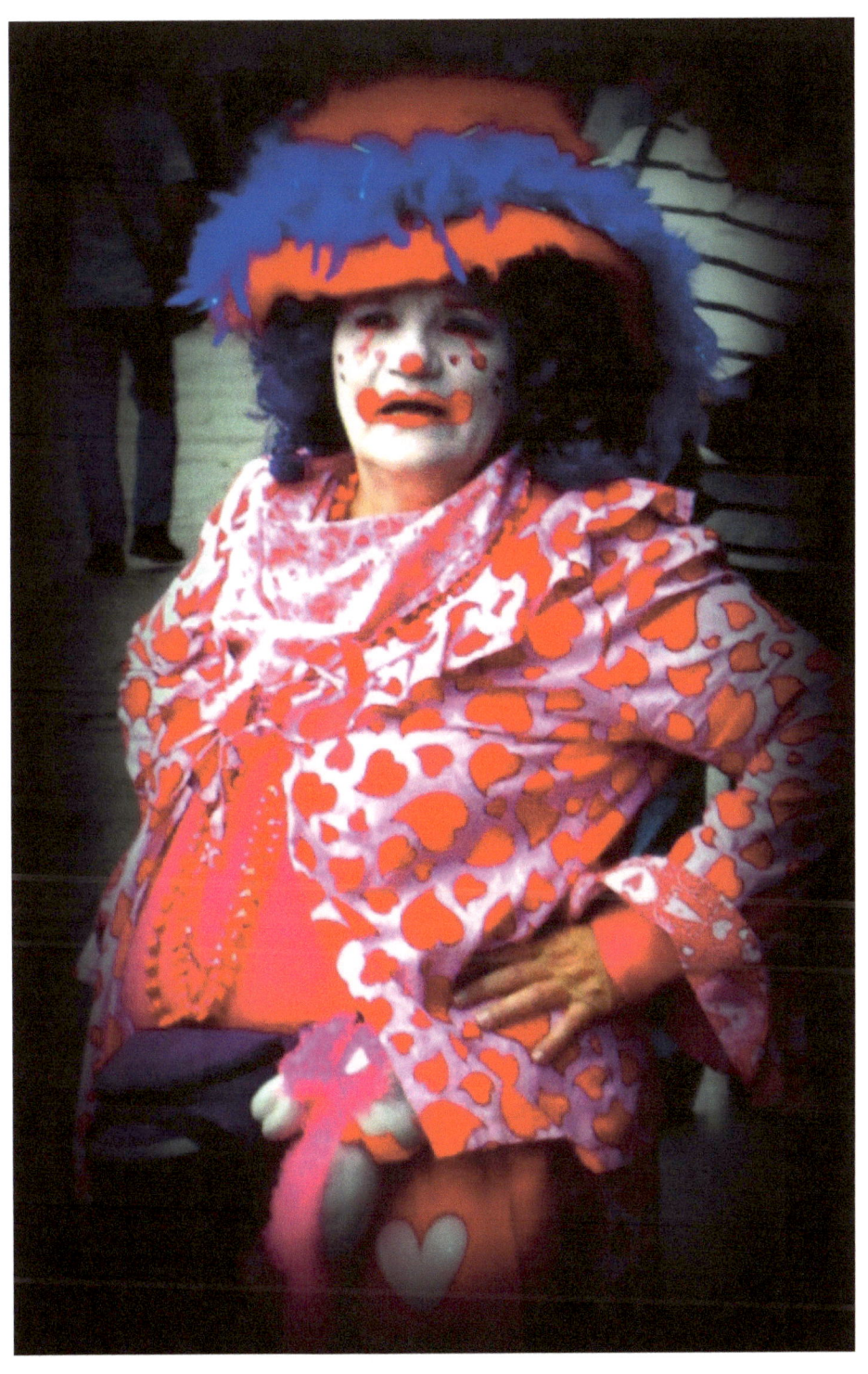

9. Only in New Orleans

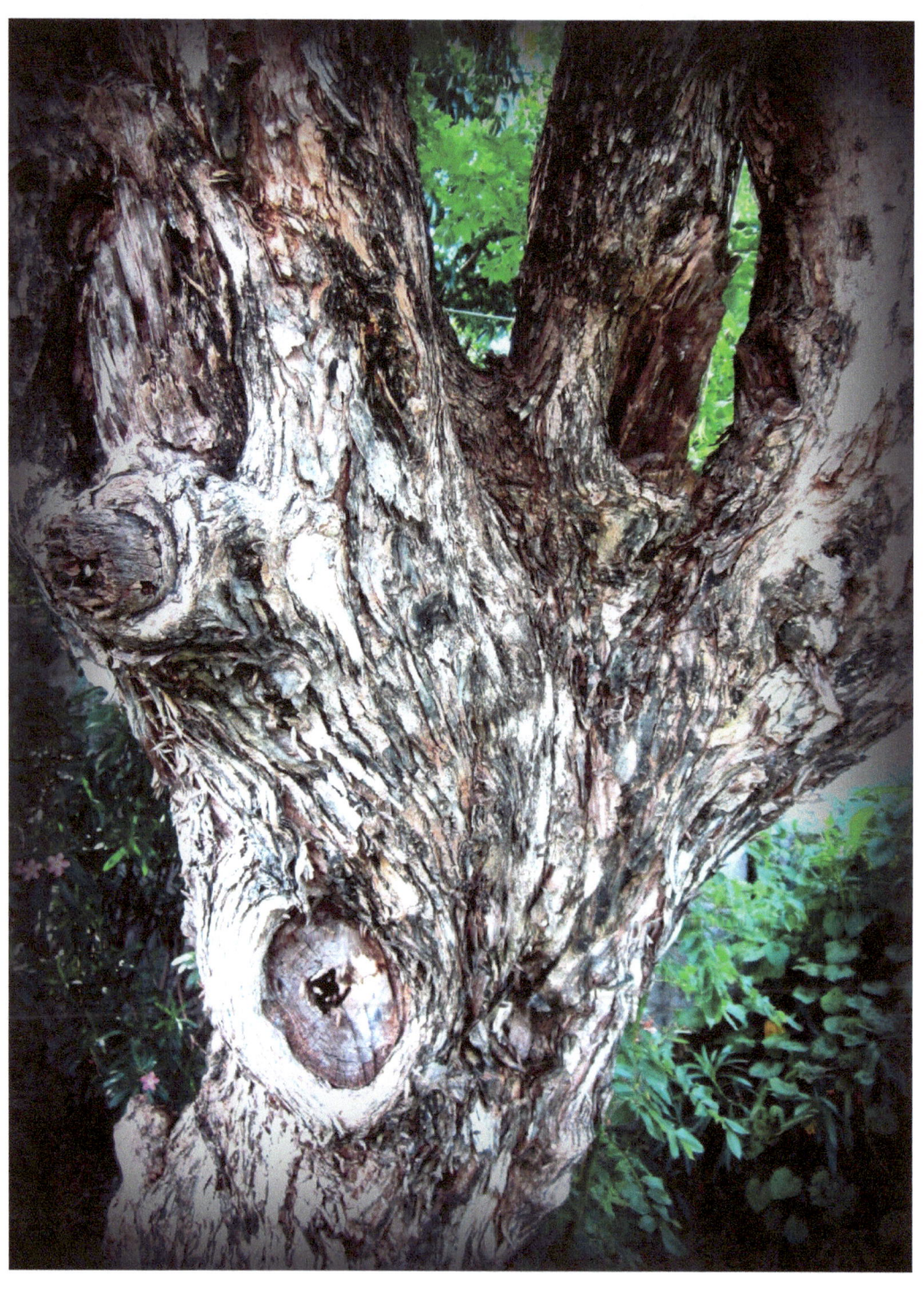

10. A Knotty Subject

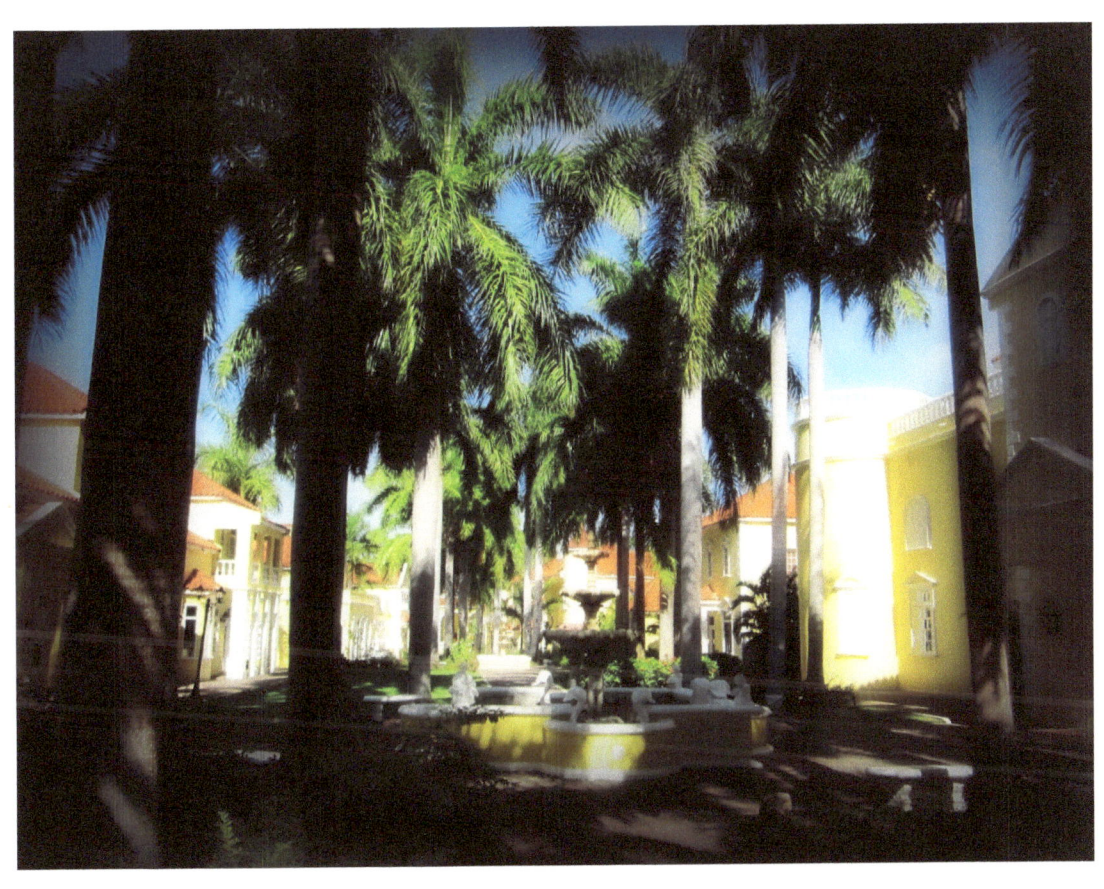

11. A Quiet Backstreet in Jamaica

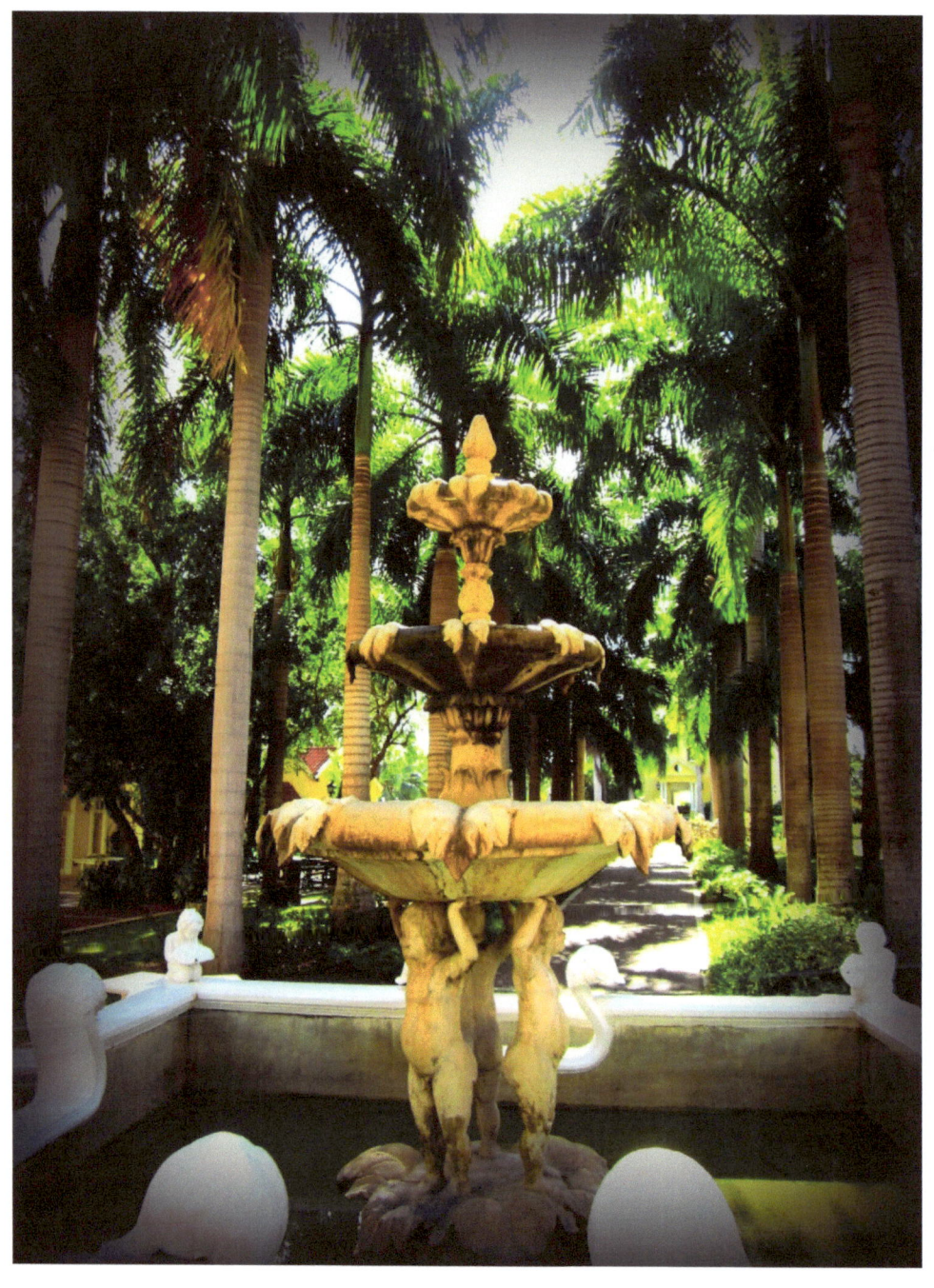

12. A Fountain of Youth in Jamaica

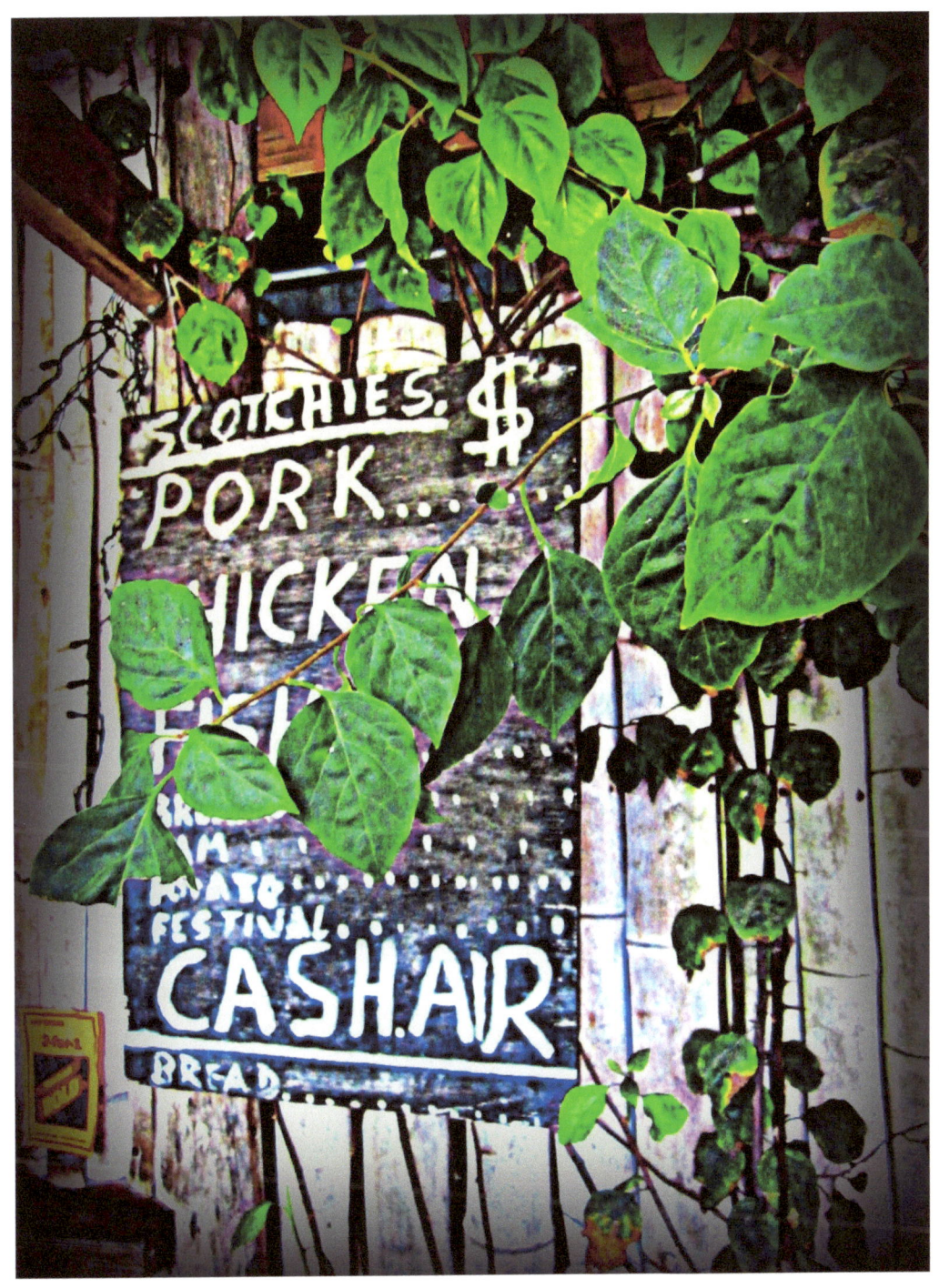

13. A Little Lunch at Scotchies, Jamaica

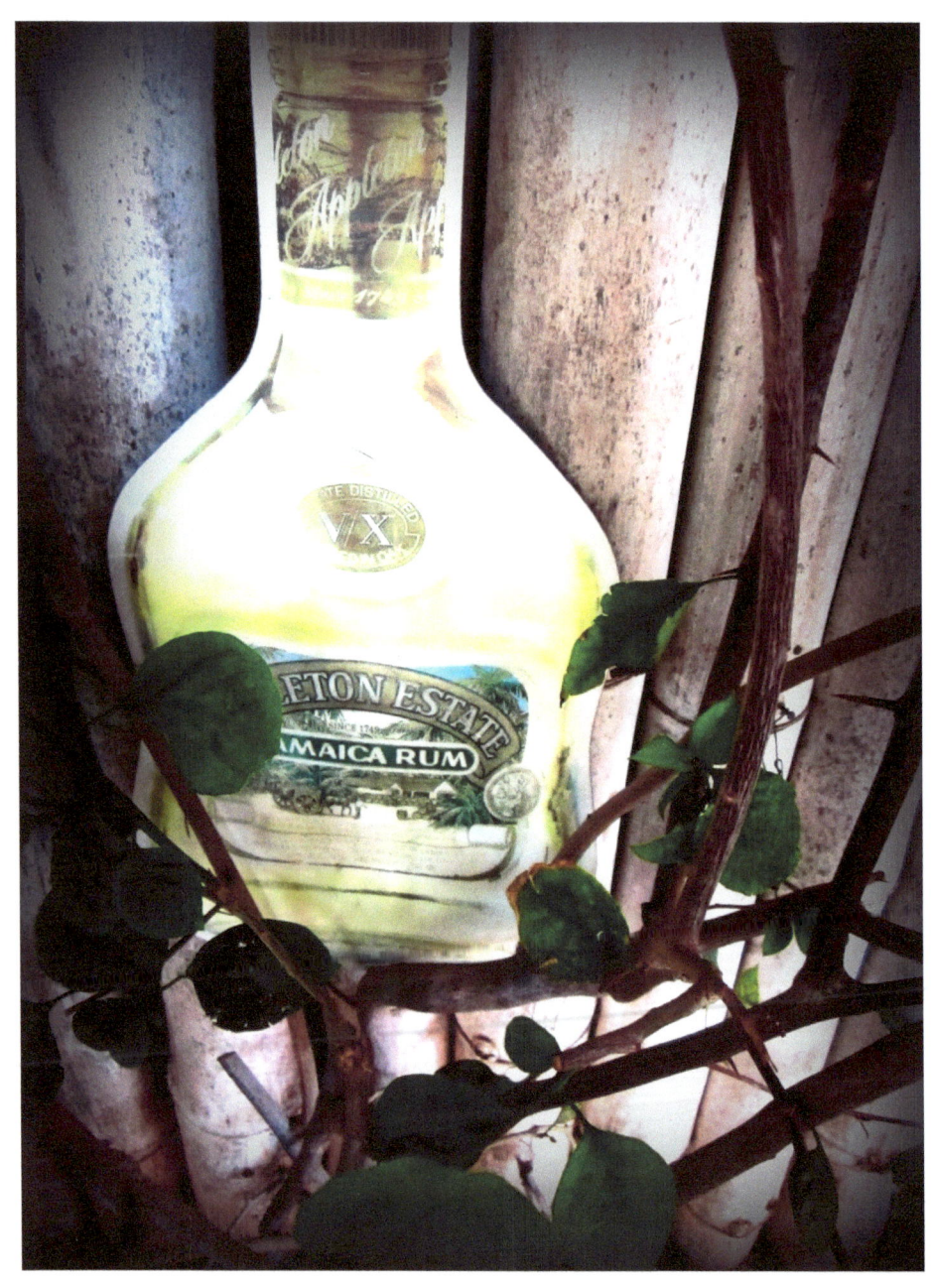

14. A Small Moistener?

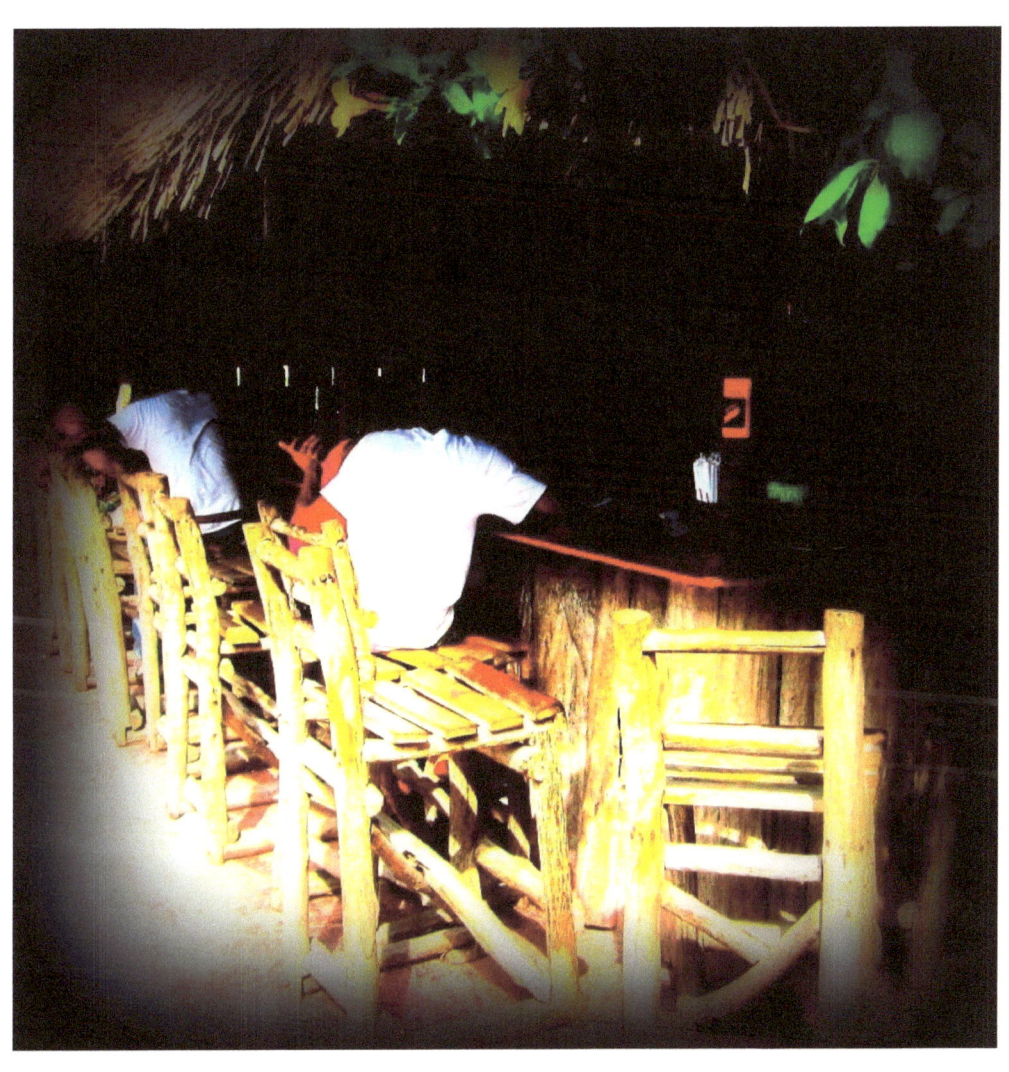

13. Secret Liaisons in Jamaica

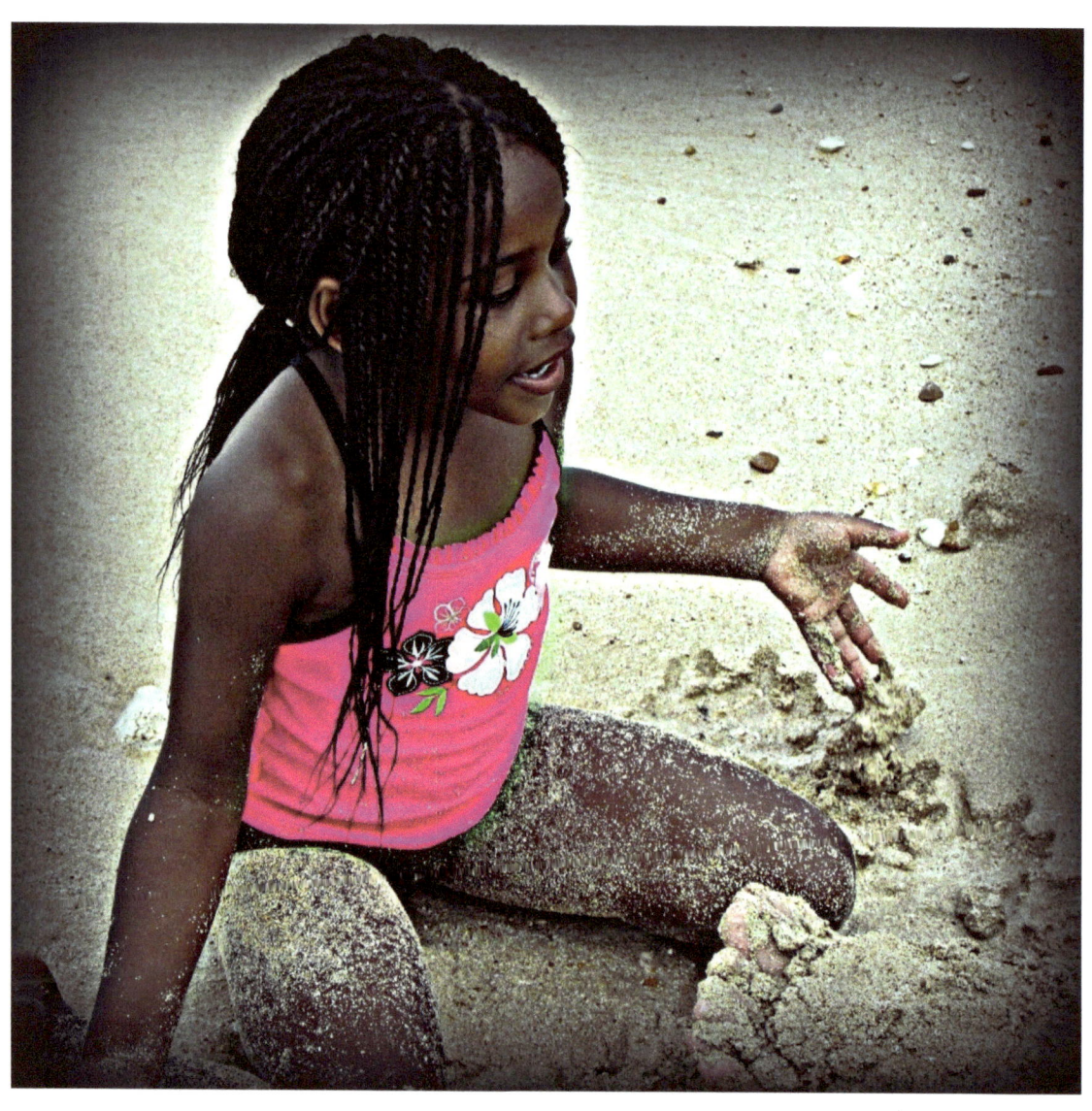

14. Young Lady on a Beach in Mexico

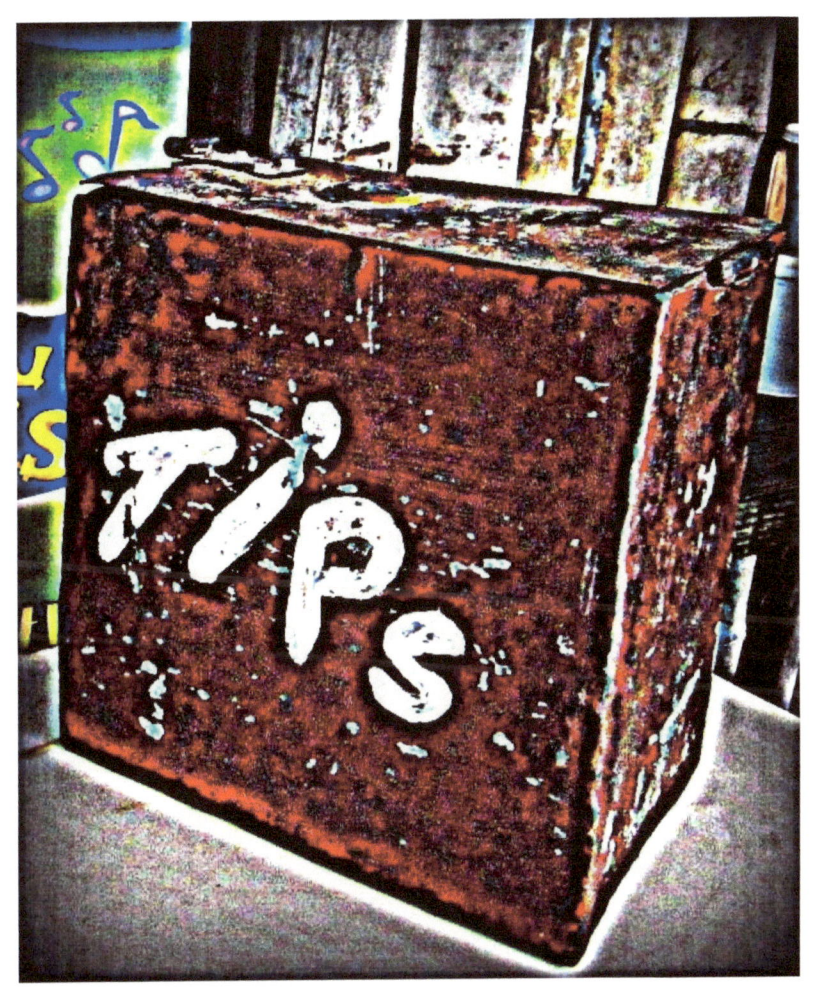

15. (1) Buy Low Sell High (2) Don't Eat the Mayonnaise You Find in a Motel Refrigerator

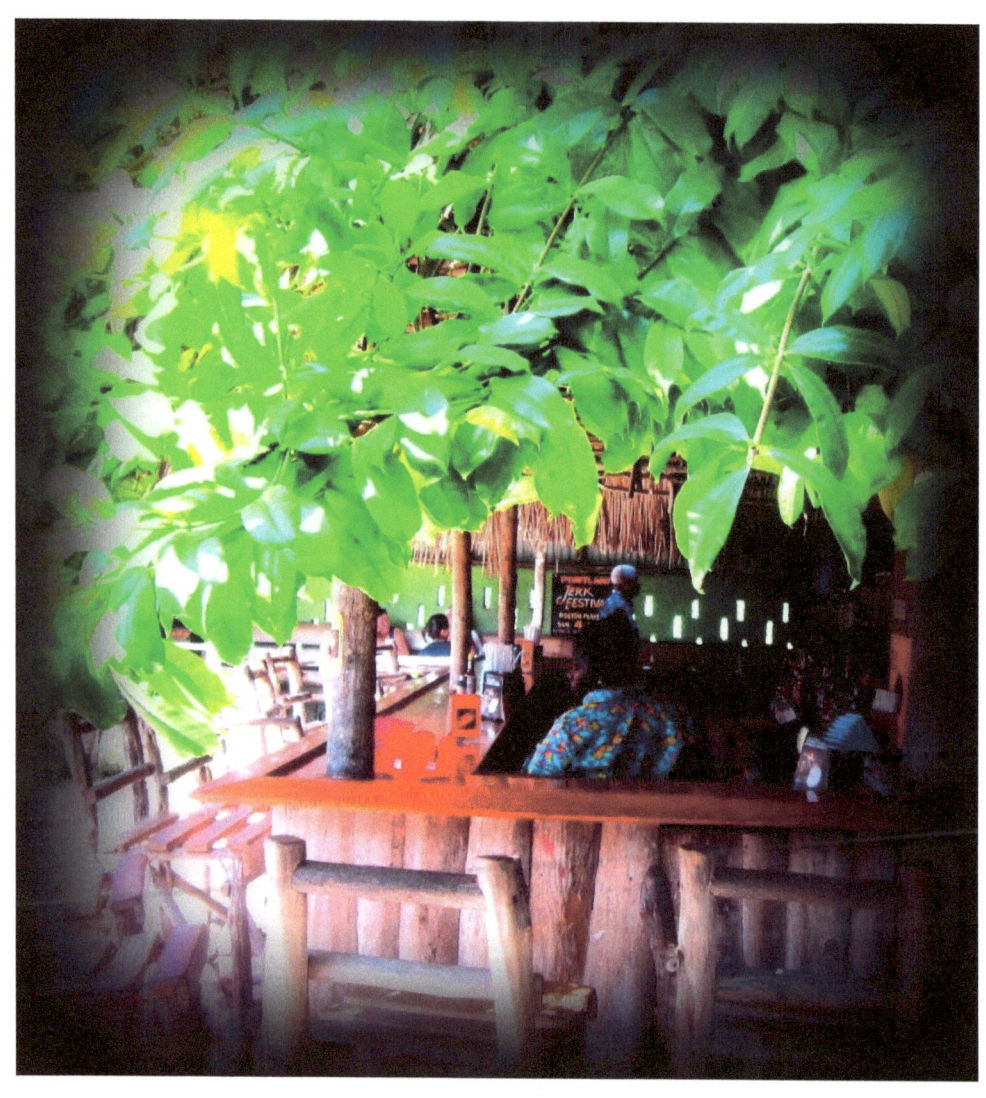

16. Waiting for the Portland Jerk Festival

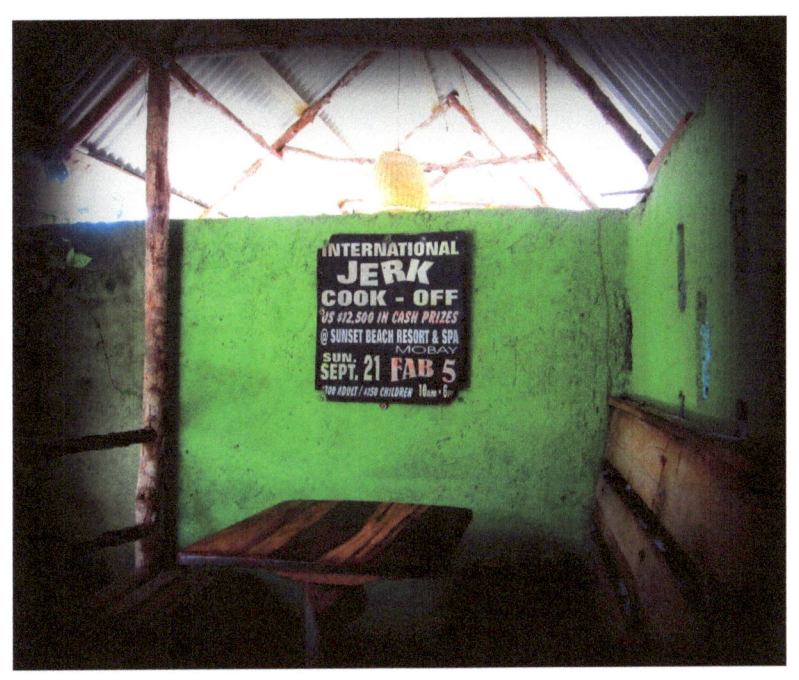

17. Anticipating a Thrilling Semi-Final

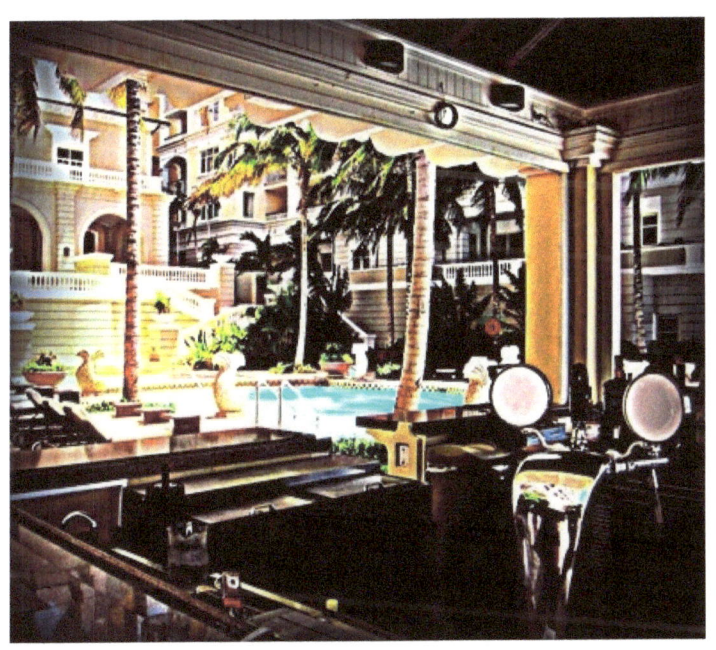

18. Nice Digs in Jamaica

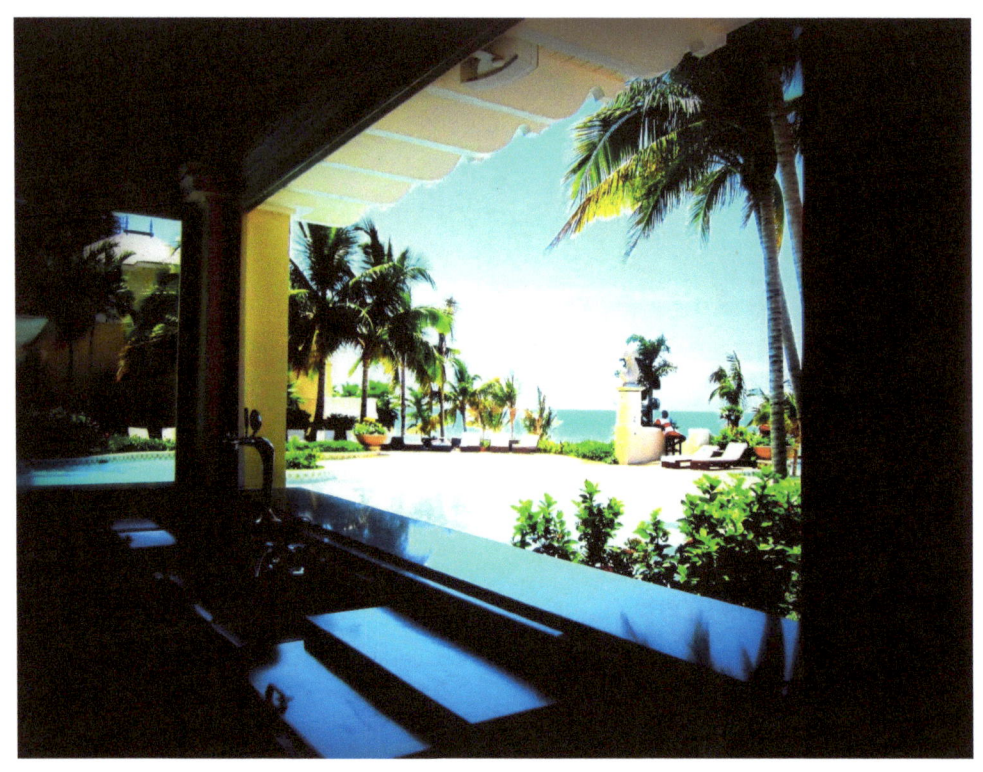

19. A Fine View from our Suite in Jamaica

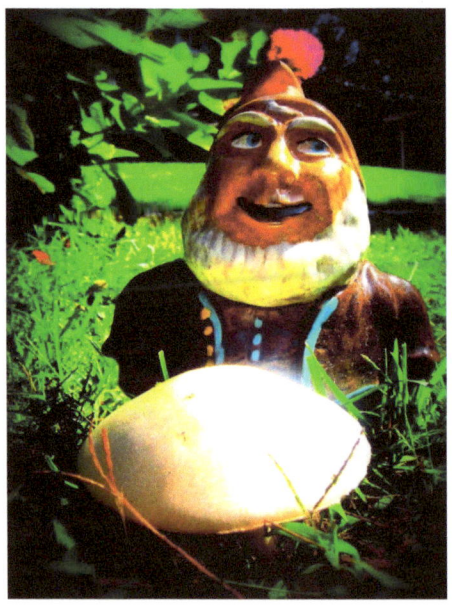

20. Gnomby – My Special Chum

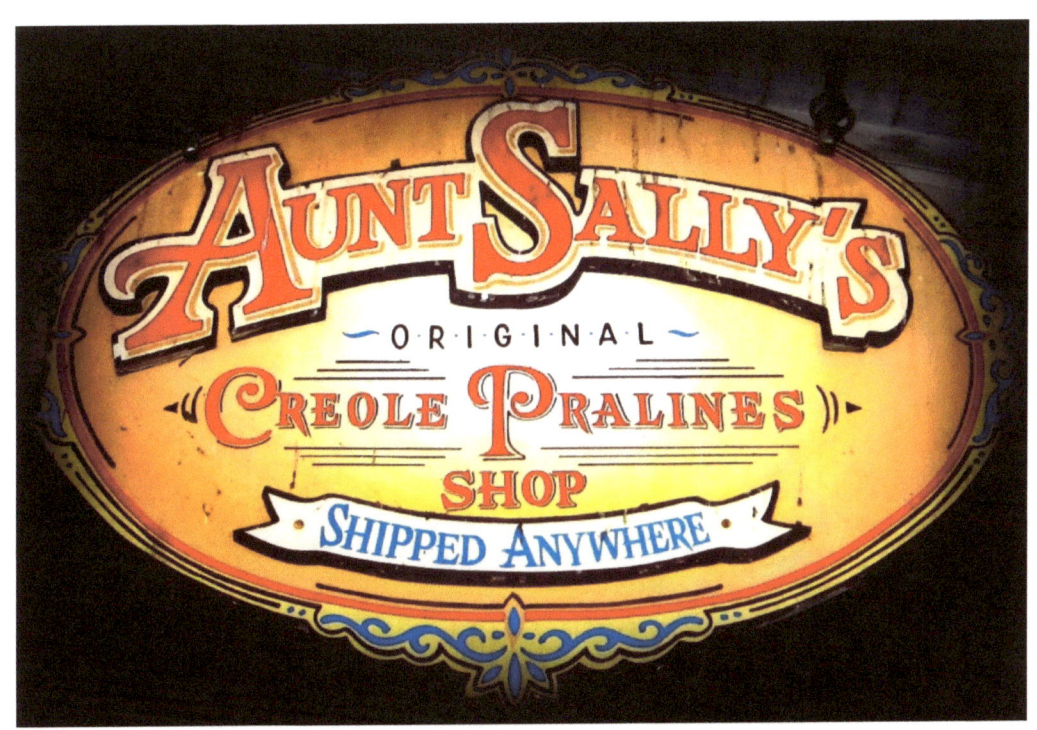

21. Going Nuts in New Orleans

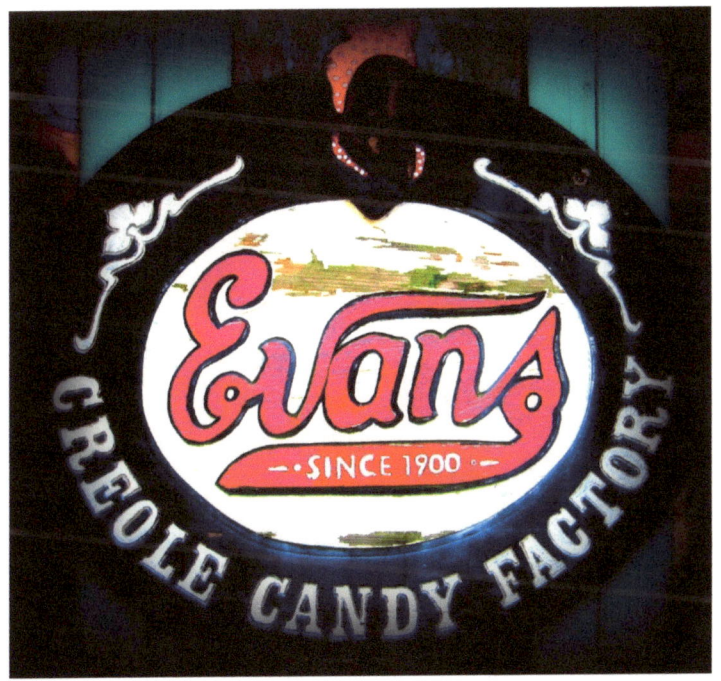

22. Evans' Creole Candy, New Orleans

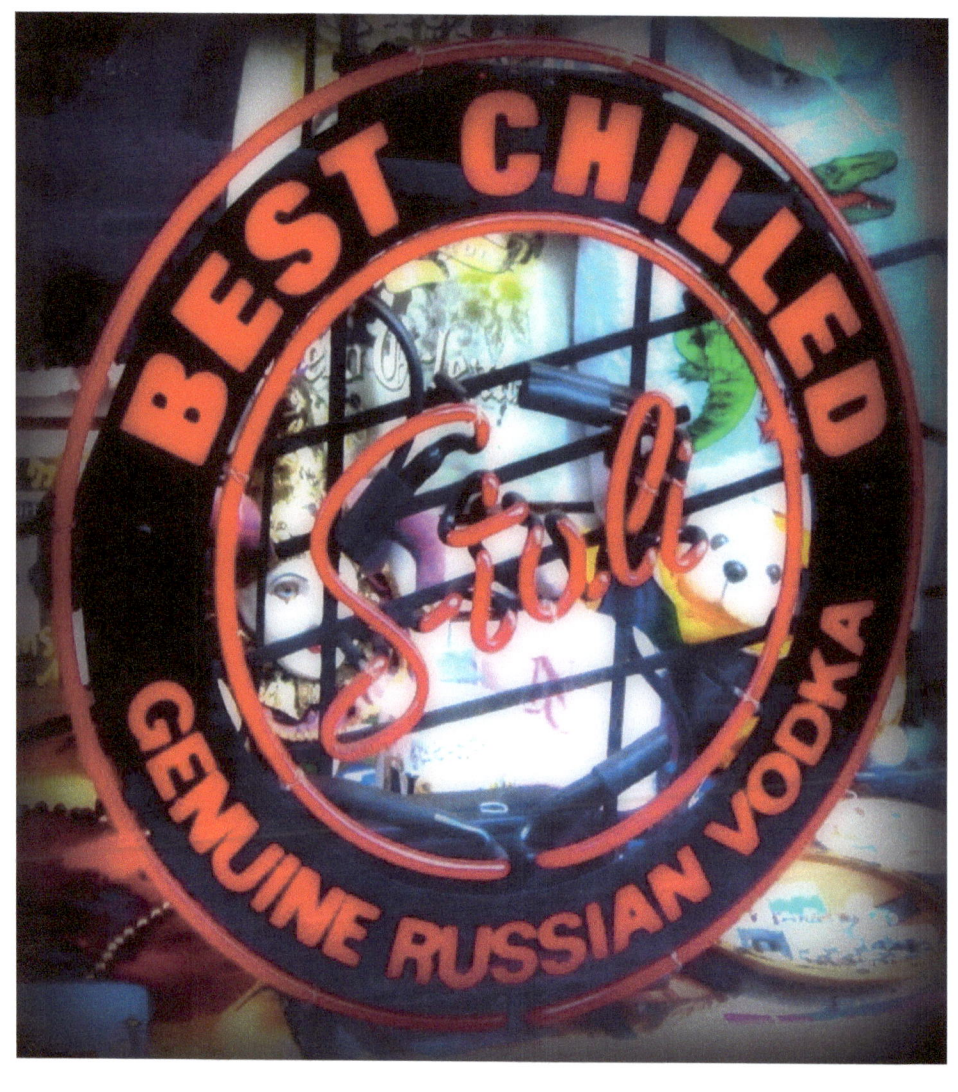

23. Could it be Bugged?

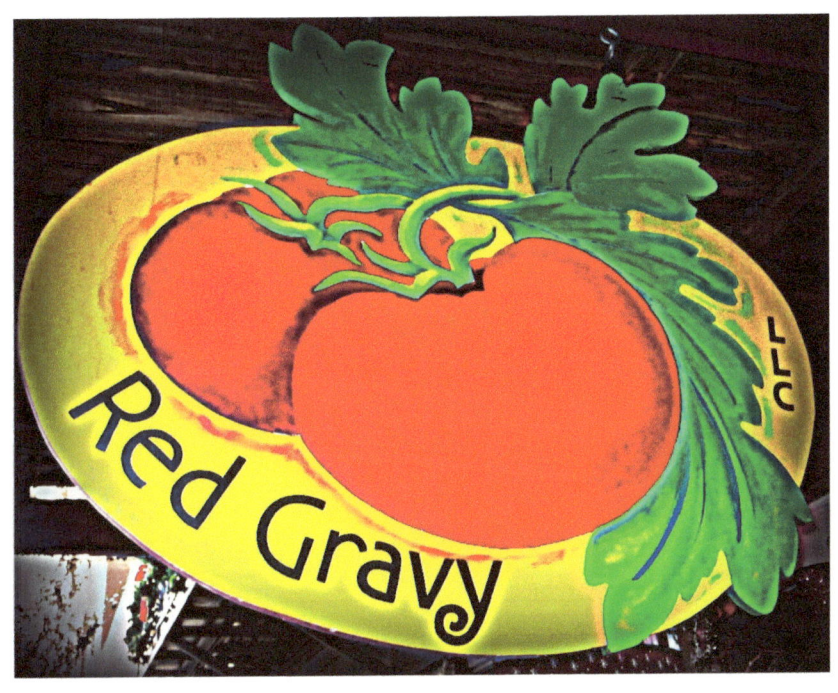

24. New Orleans Famous Red Gravy (Links to the White House?

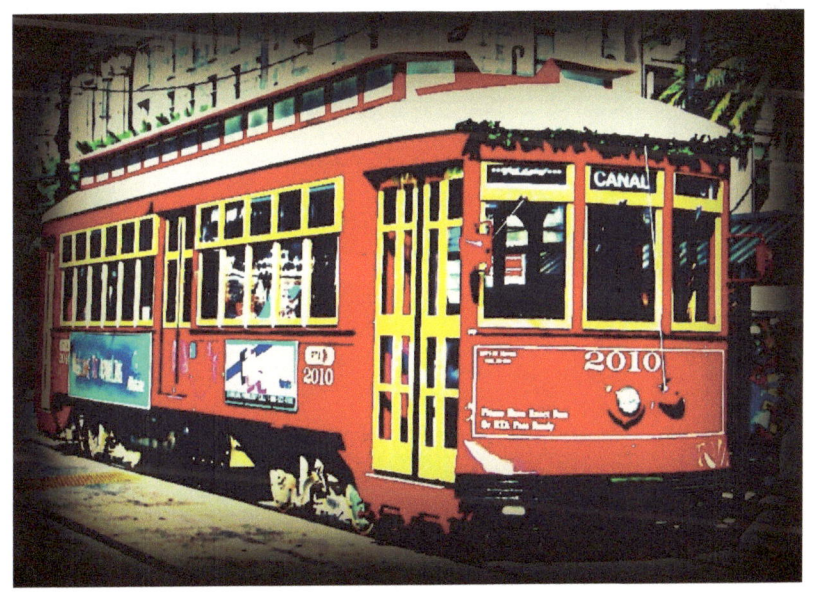

25. A Fine New Orleans Tram

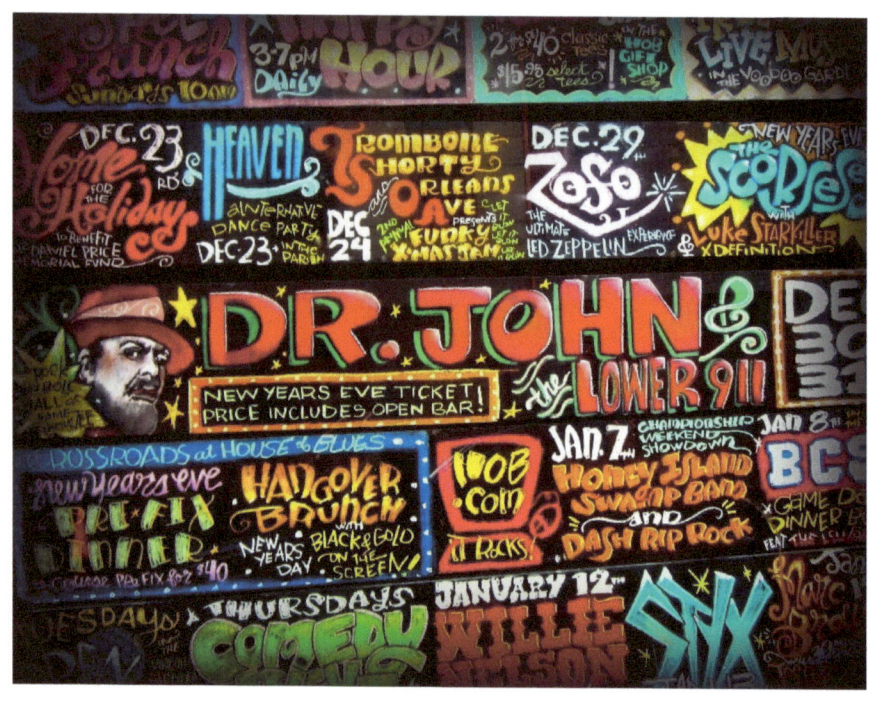

26. What's on at the House of Blues, New Orleans?

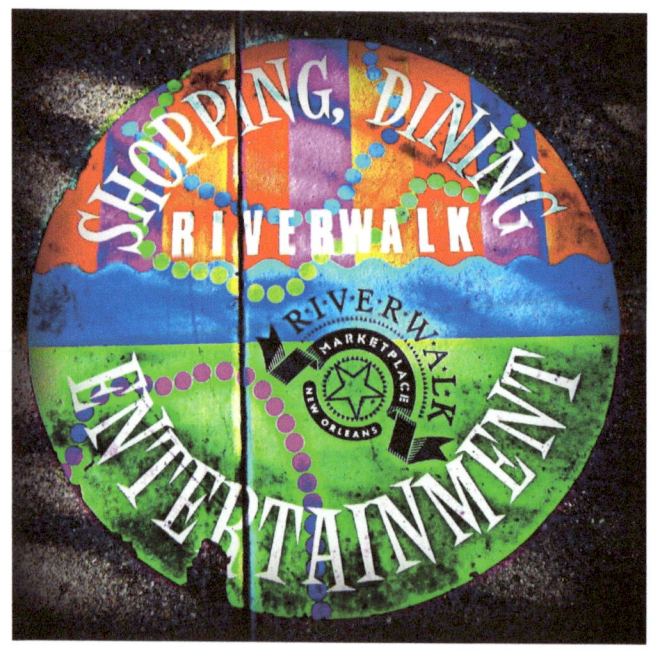

27. A Little Lunch at the Riverwalk Perhaps?

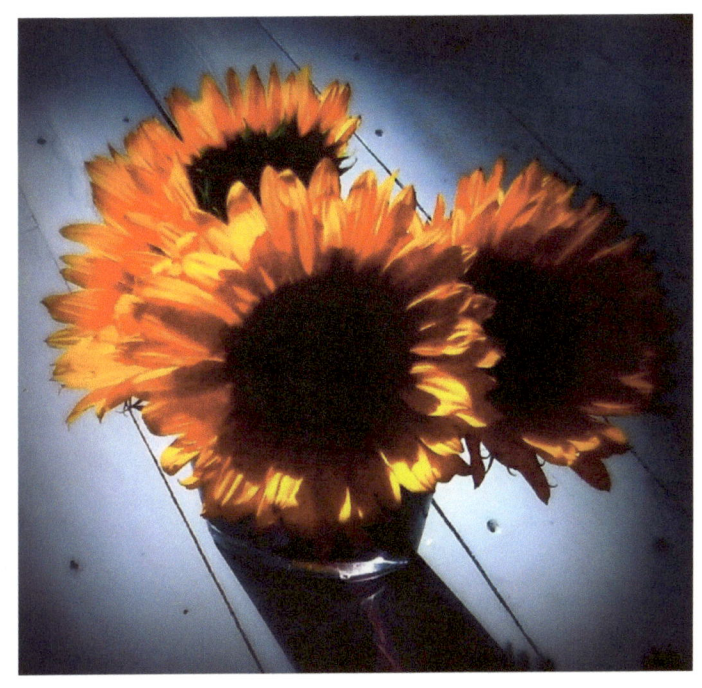

28. Californian Sunflowers

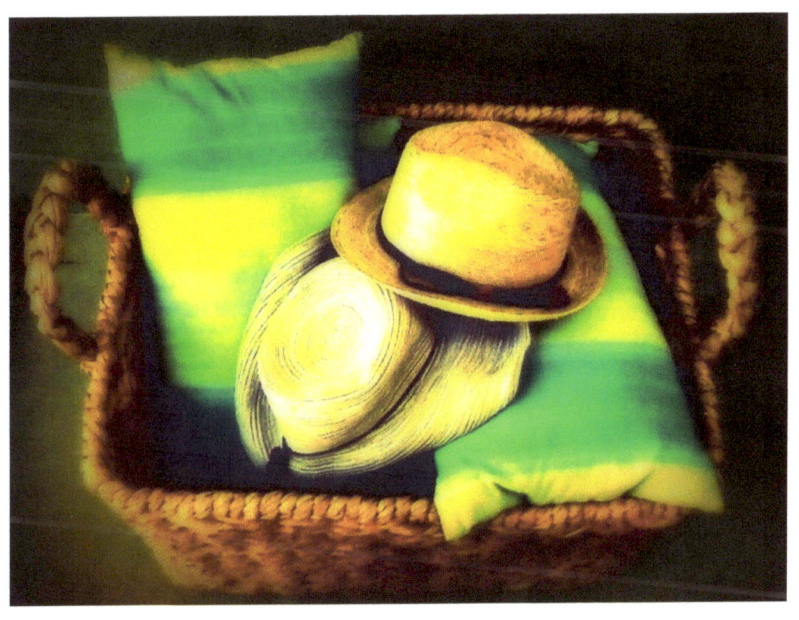

29. Hats in a Basket

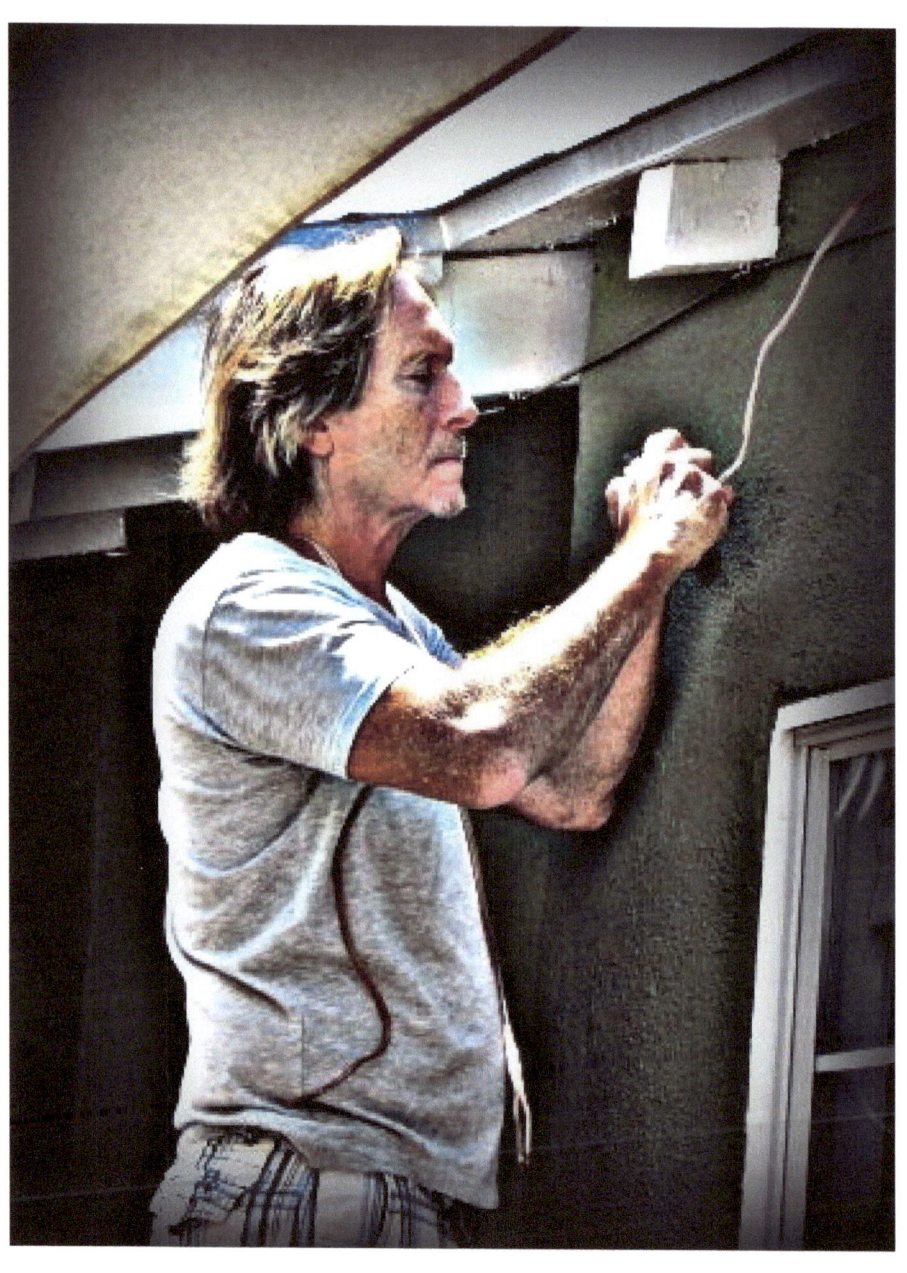

30. My Old Chum Film Director C.B. Harding Getting a Quick Fix

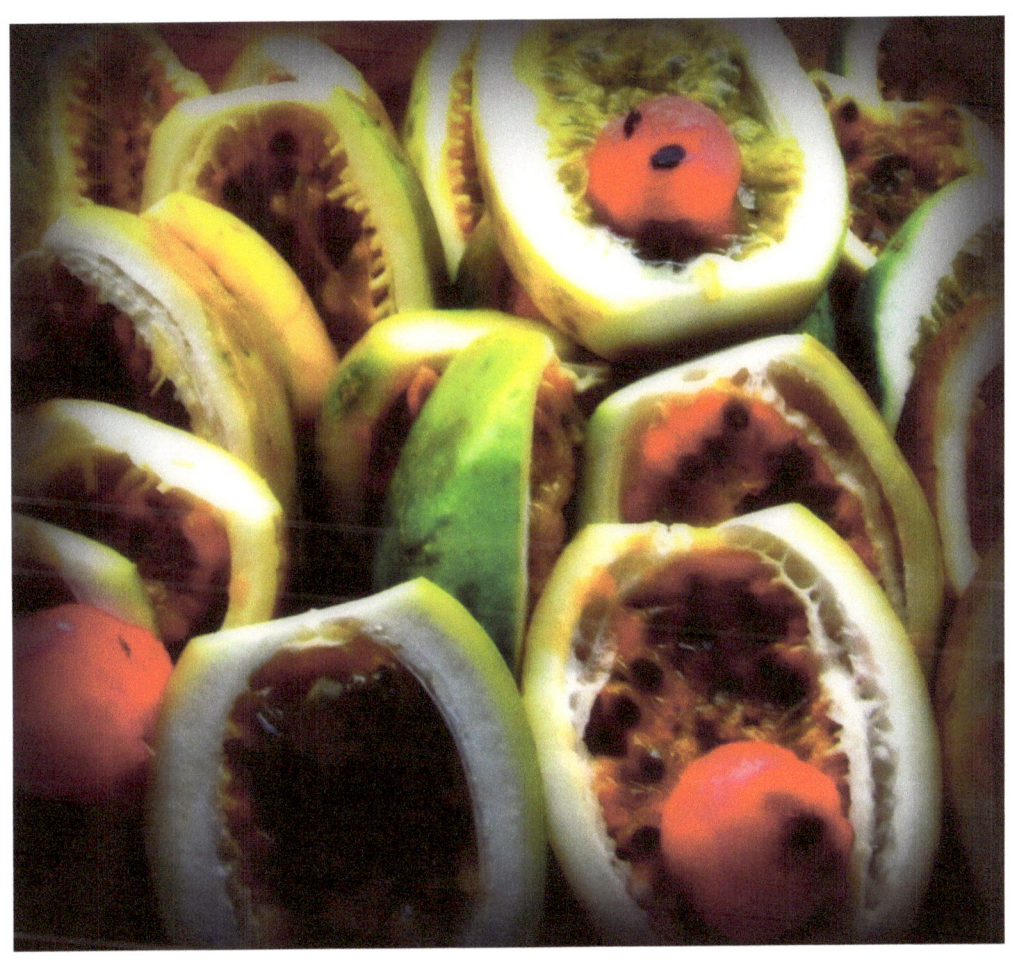

31. Hunting Phileas Fogg

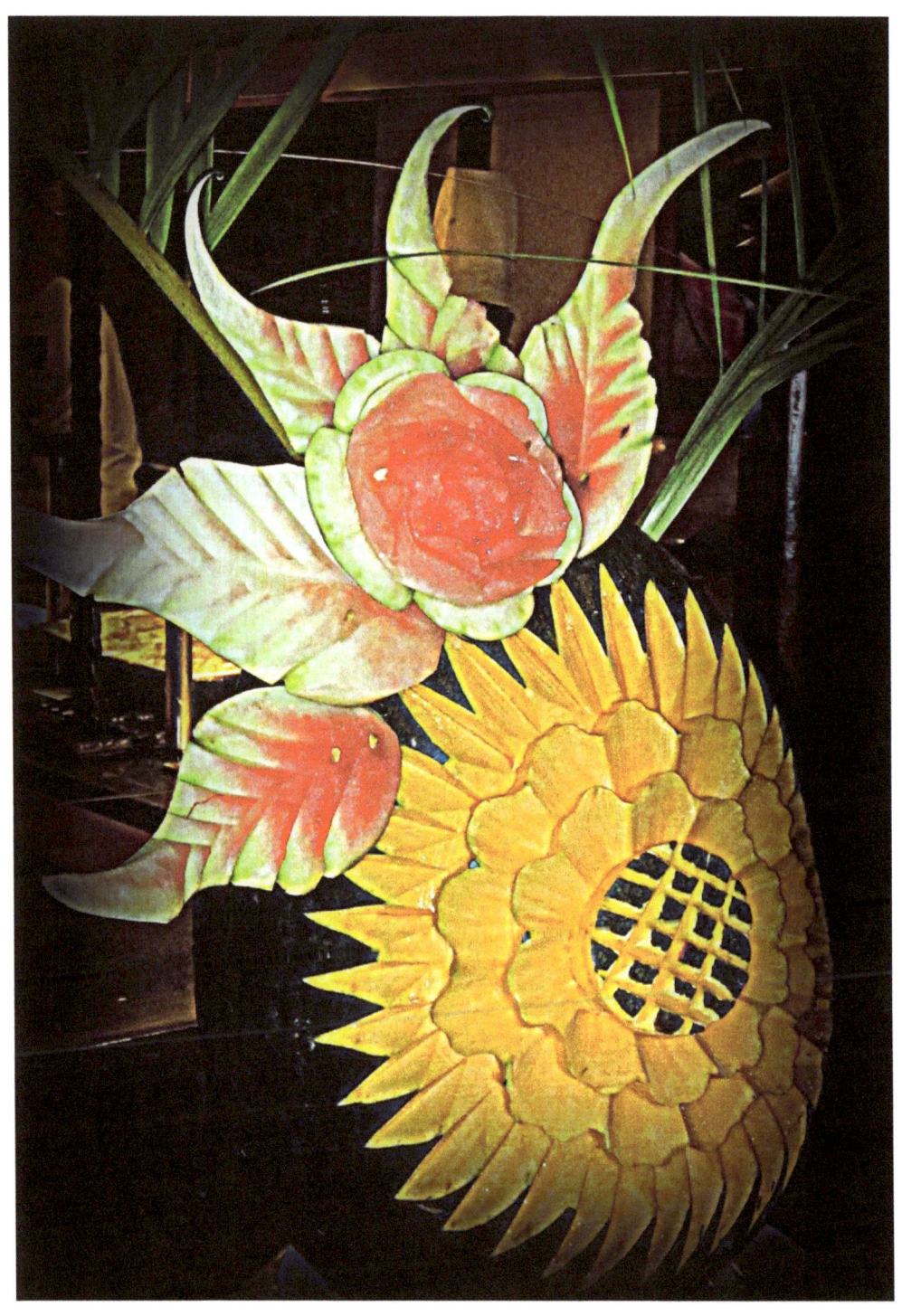

32. Not the Carnegie Mellon

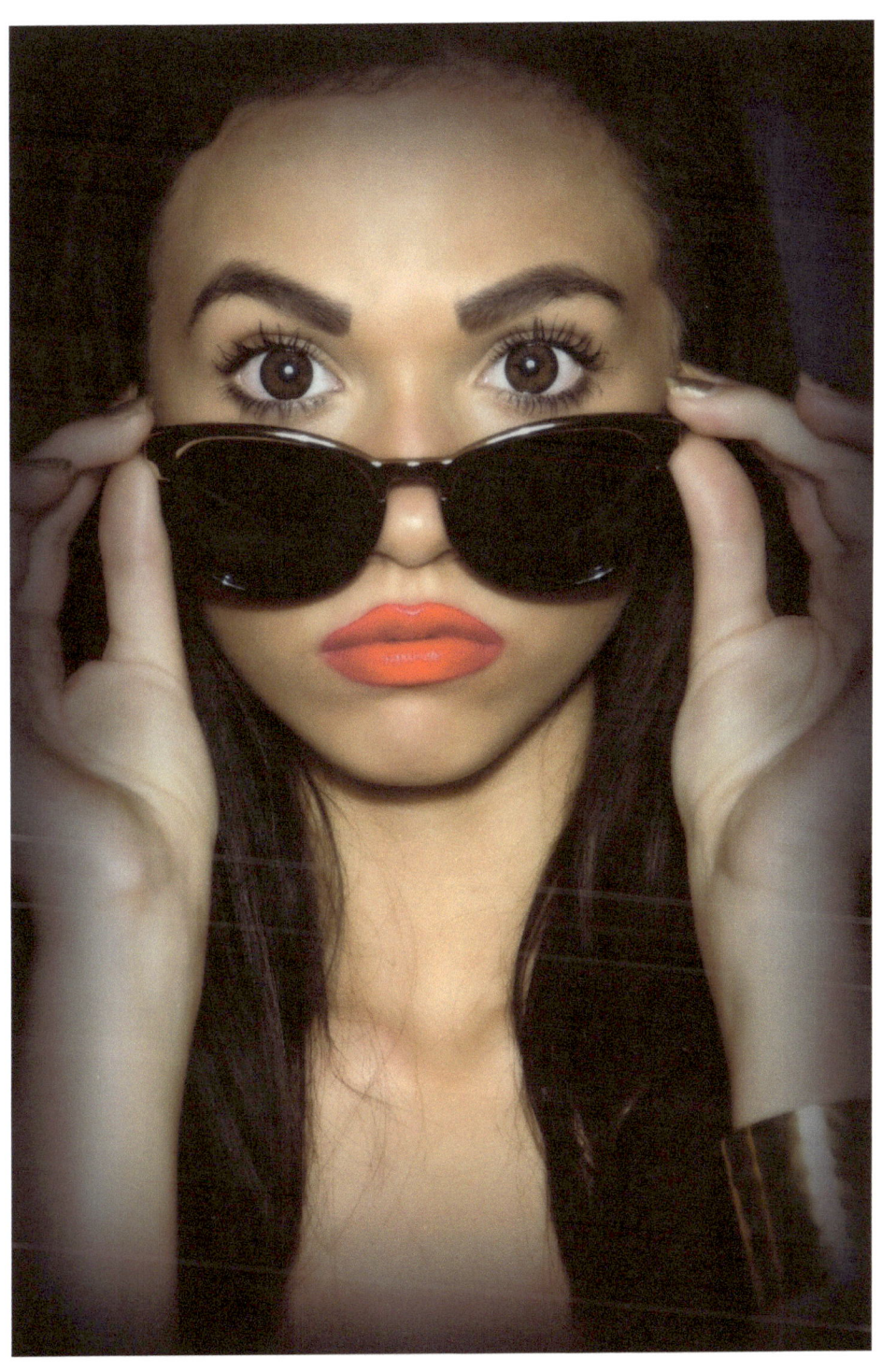

33. Alex (1)

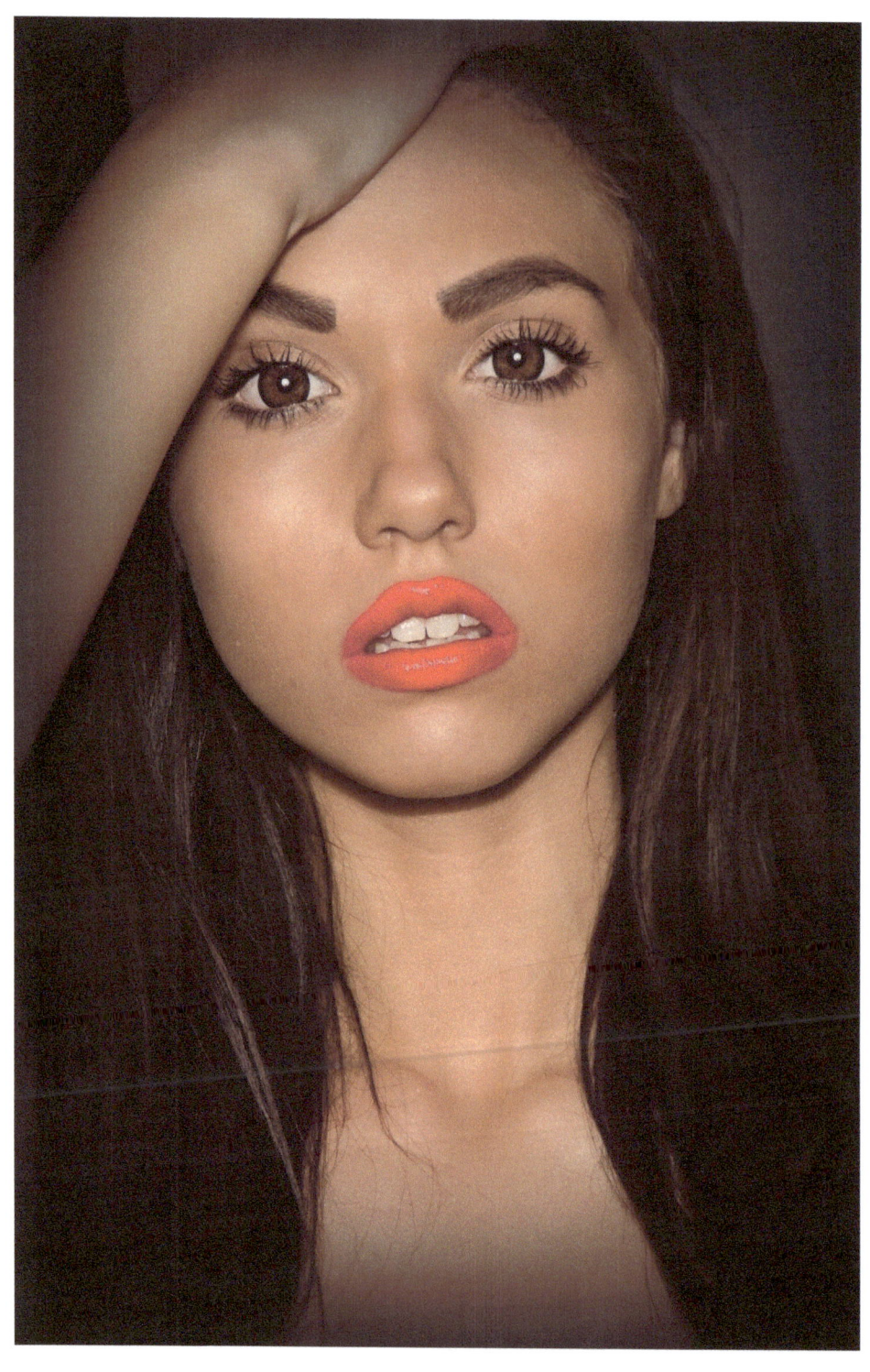

34. Alex (2)

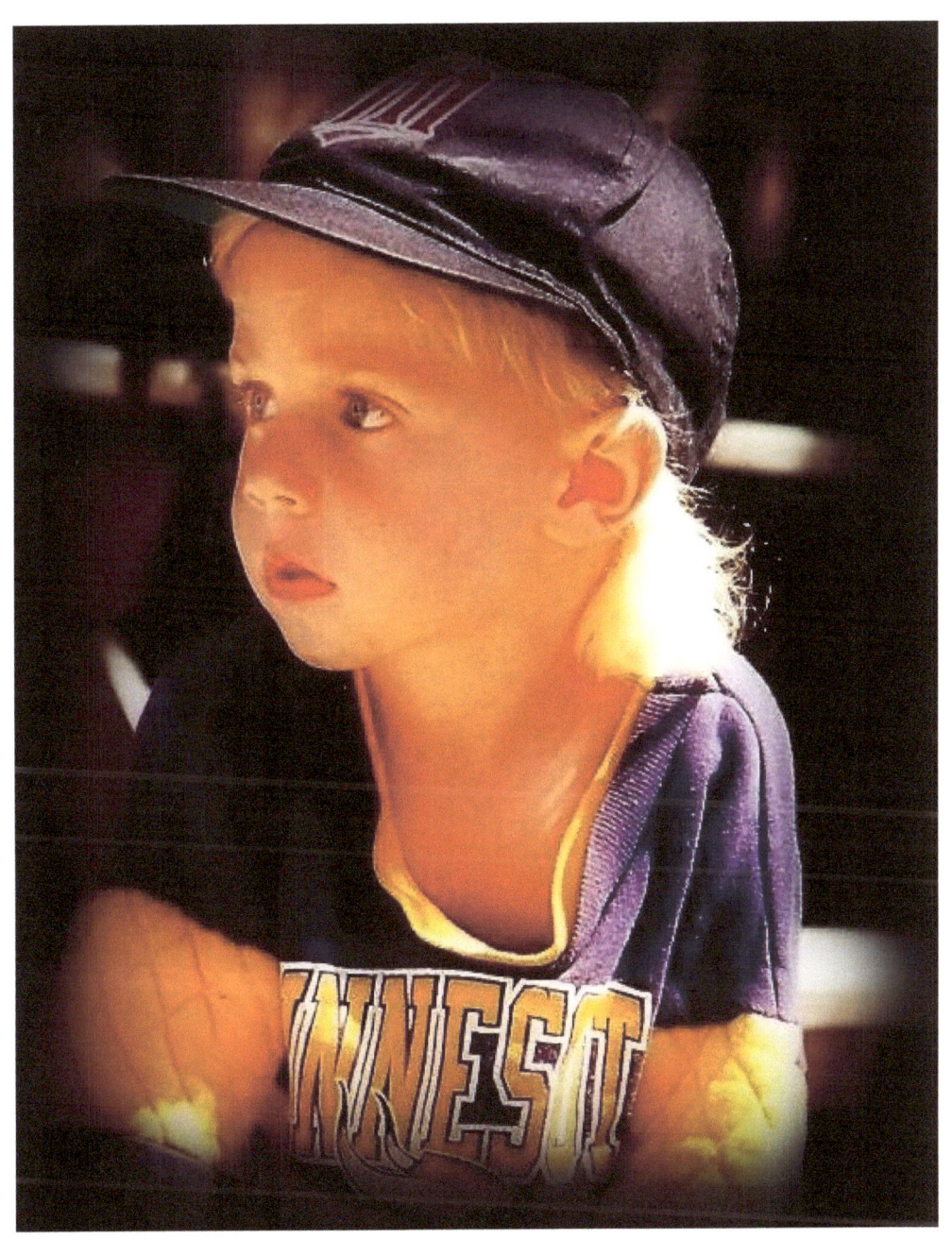

35. Jelly-Boy Pinky

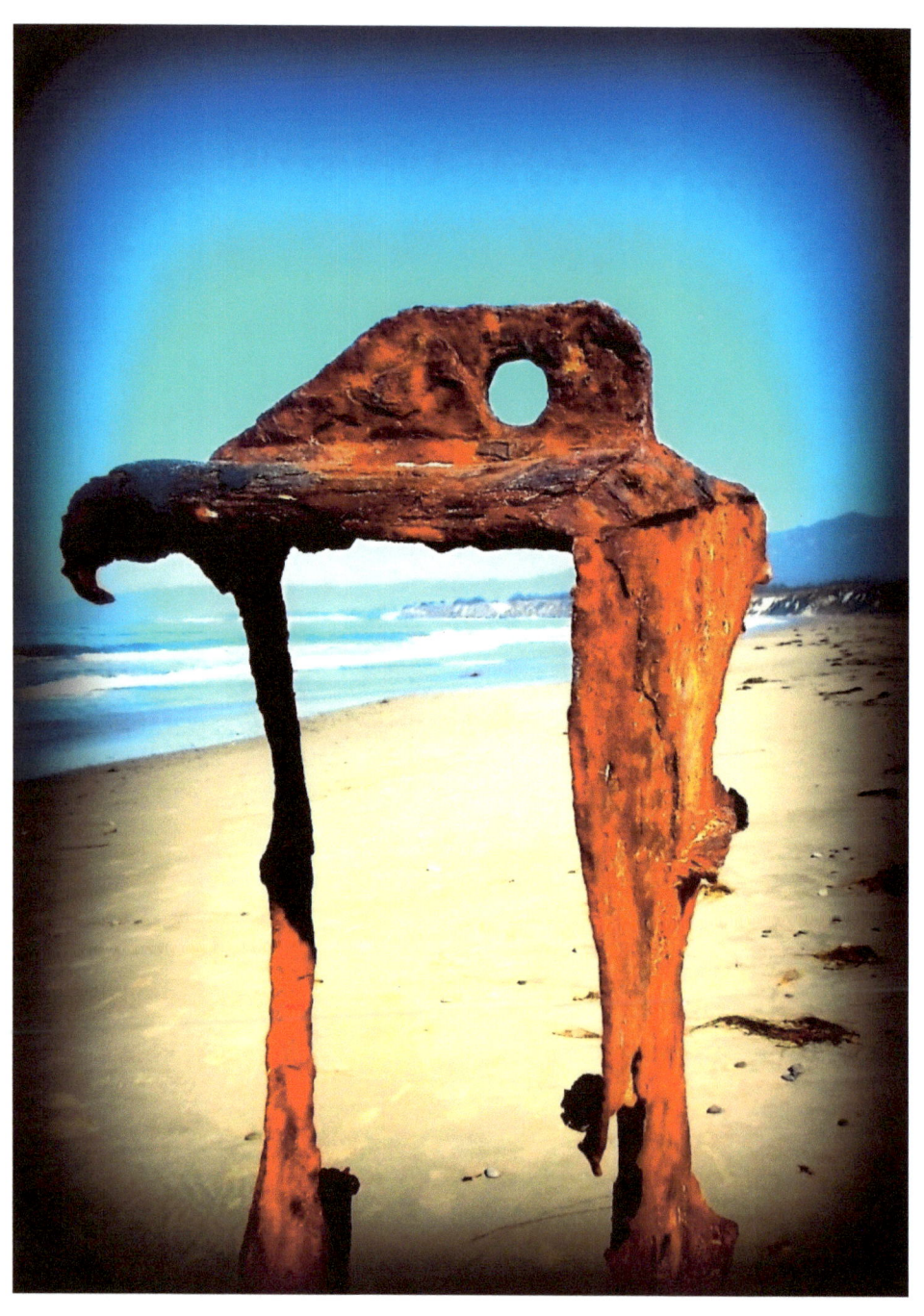

36. War of the Worlds – Santa Monica

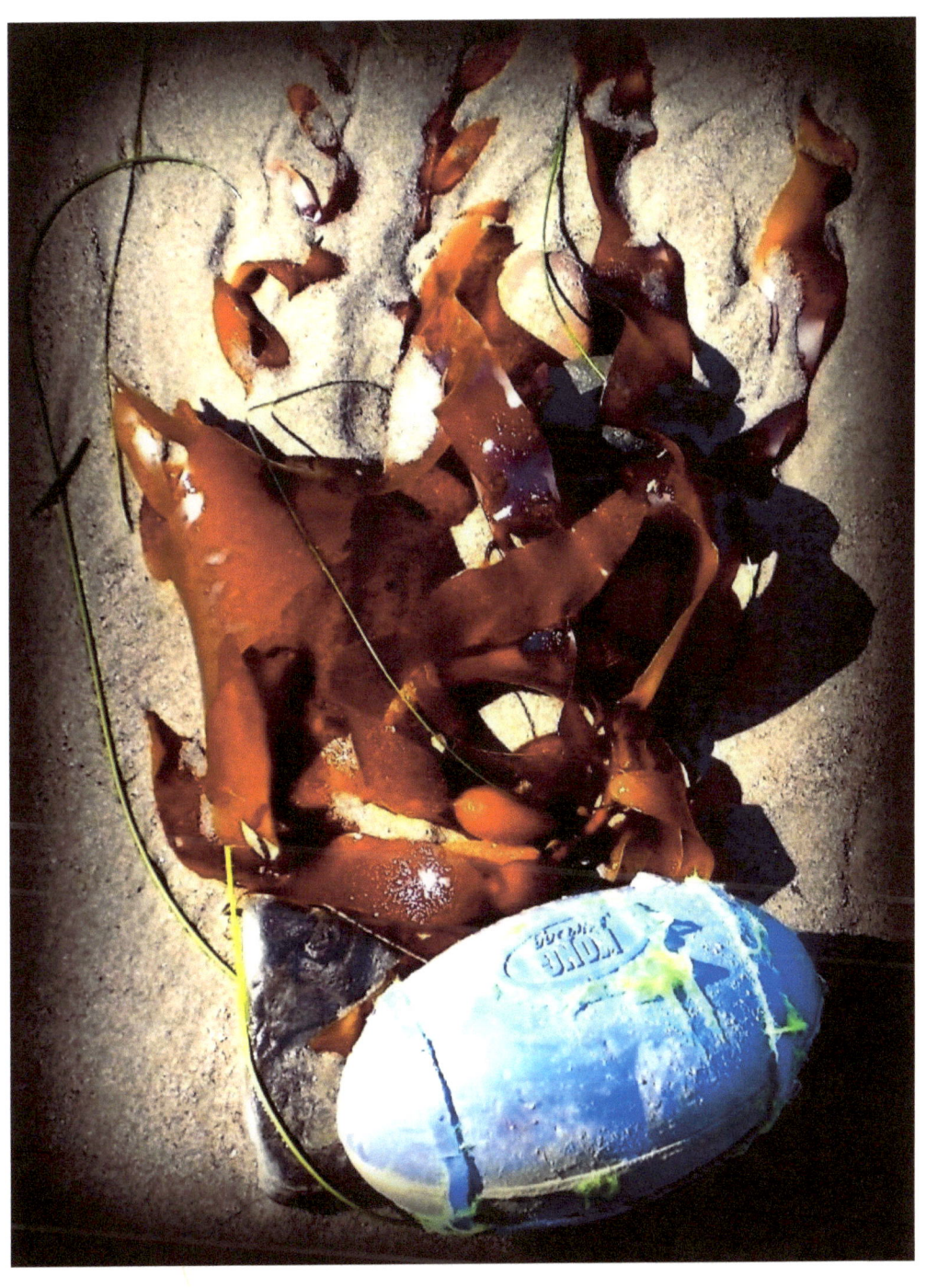

37. Seaweed Receiver

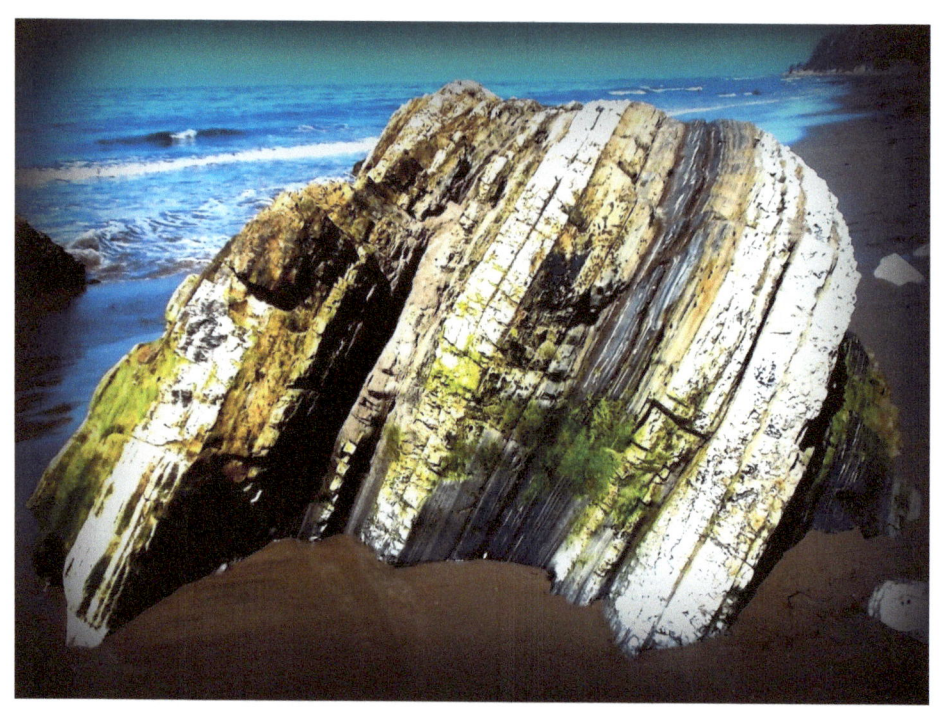

38. Rock of Ages – Goleta Beach, California

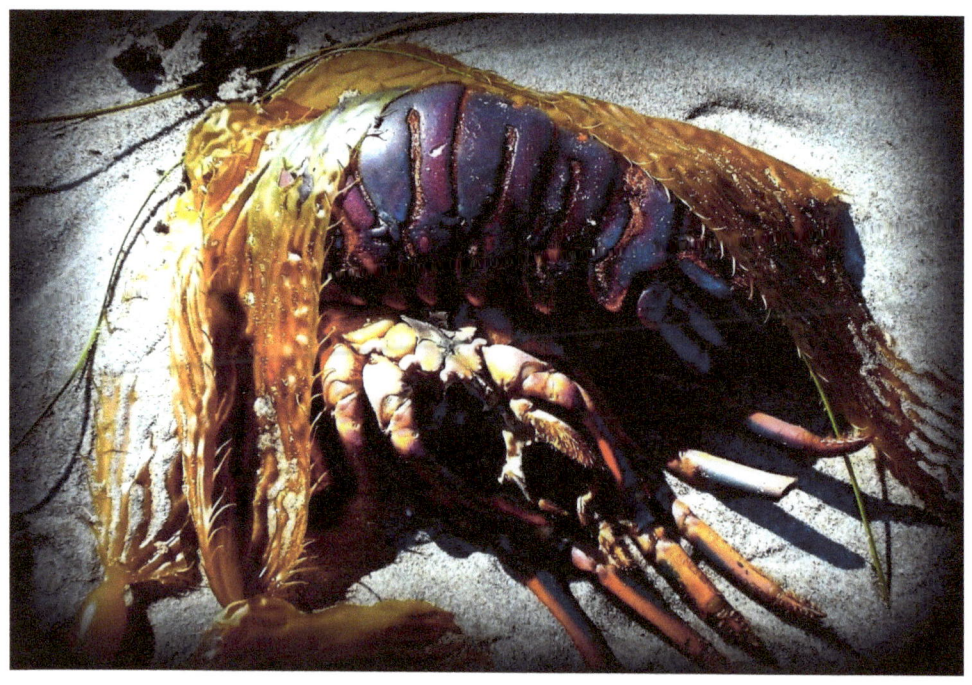

39. Lobster in Witness Protection, Goleta CA.

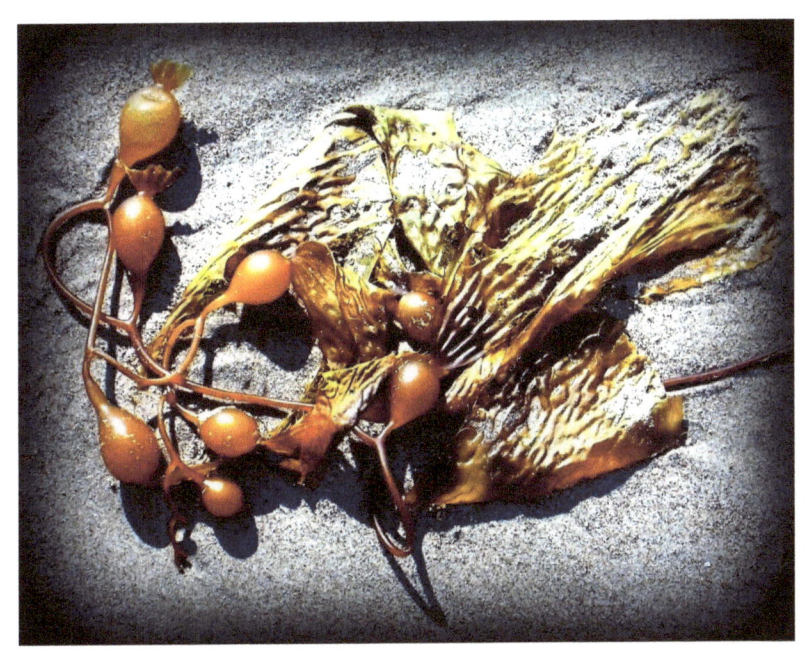

40. All Washed Up (1)

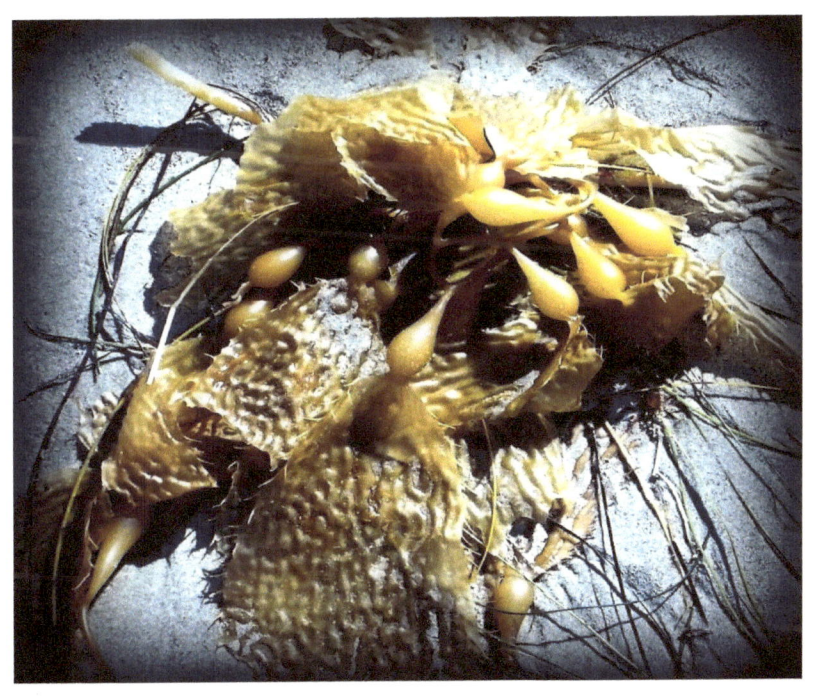

41. All Washed Up (2)

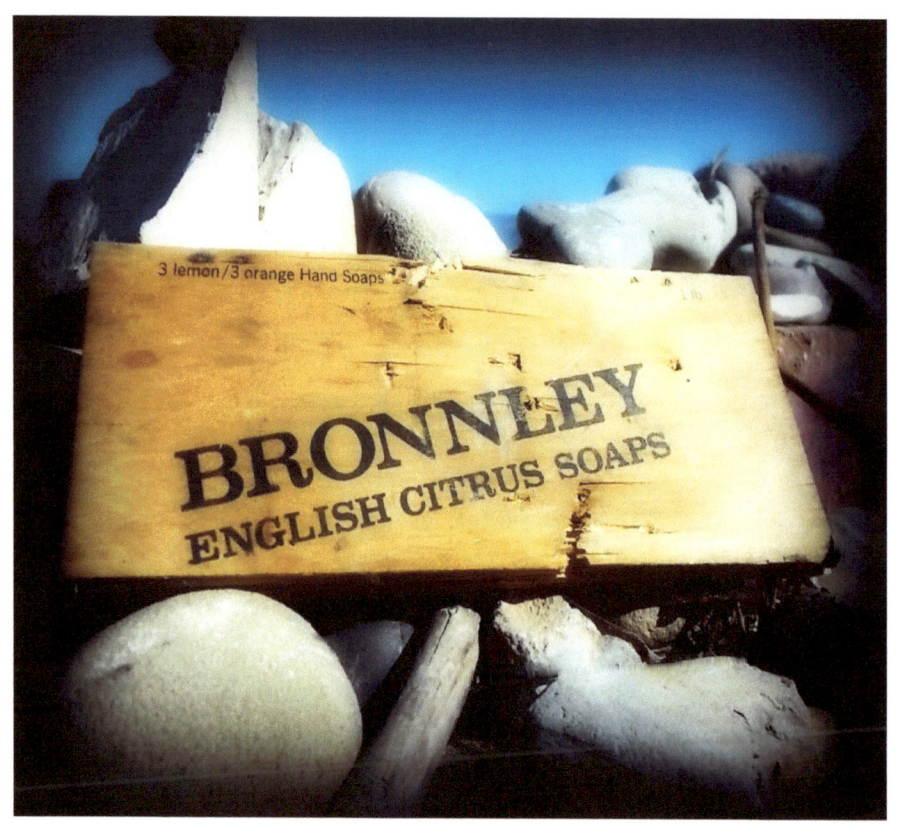

42. A Nice Clean Beach in California

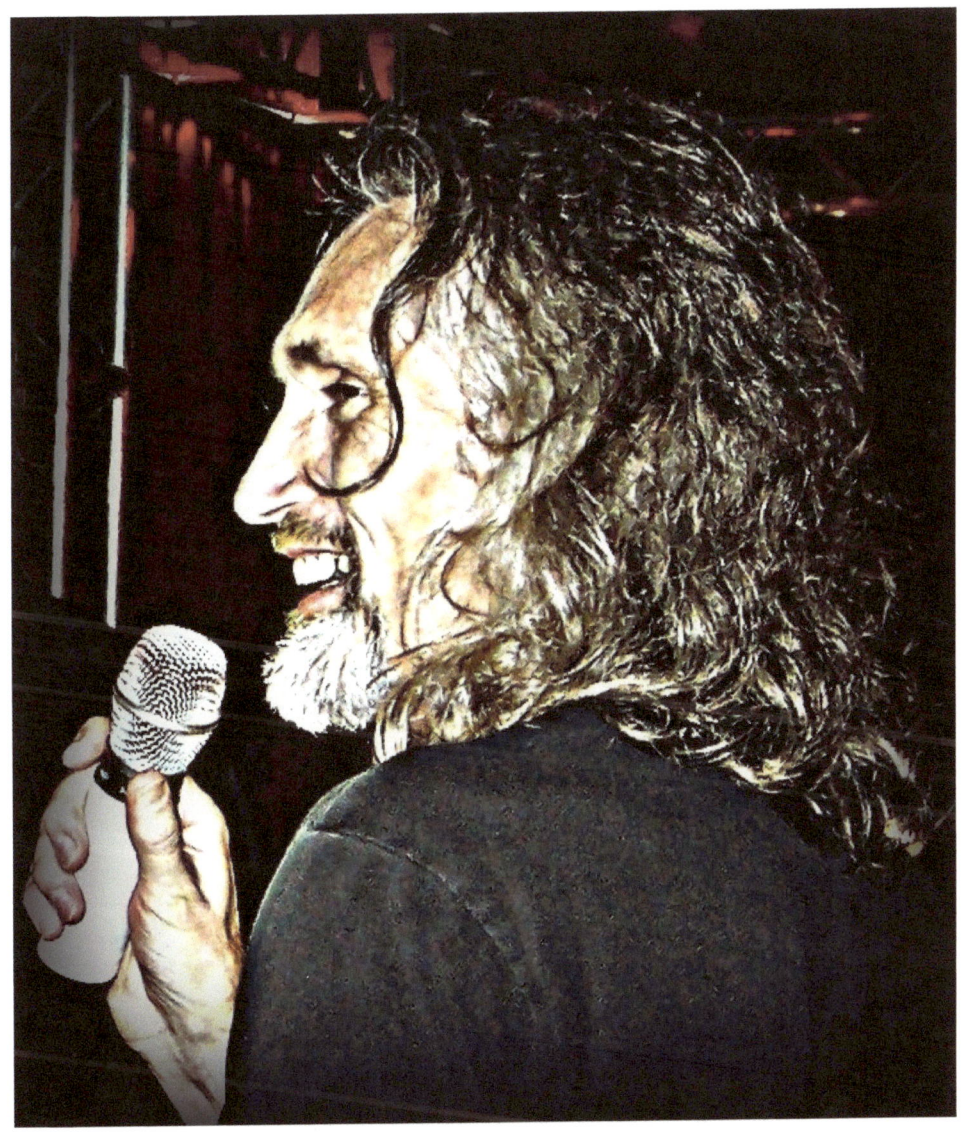

43. The Brilliant Joey Waldon

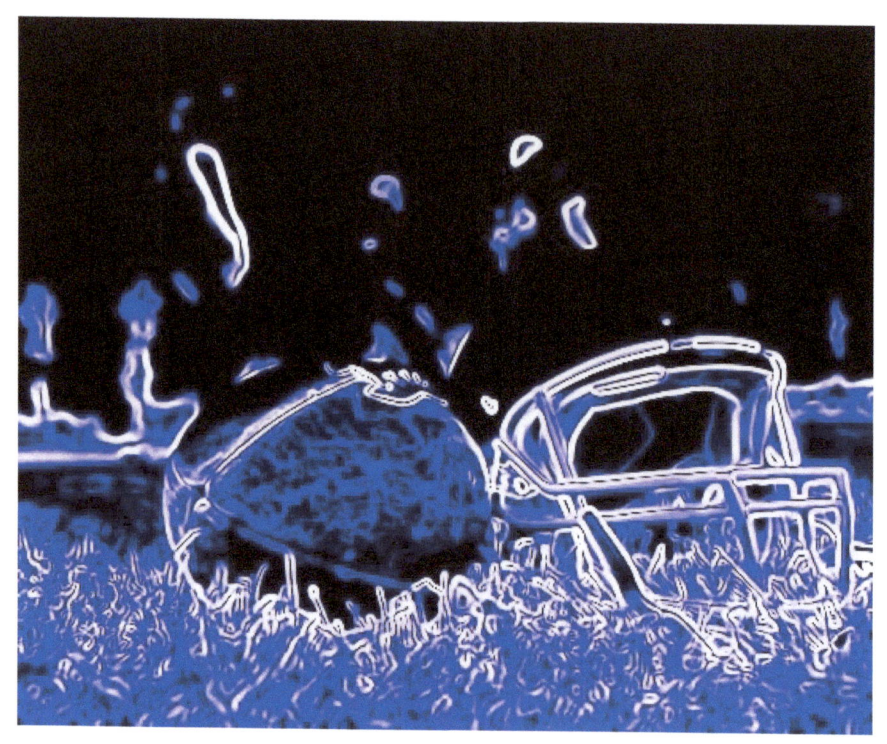

44. End of Season

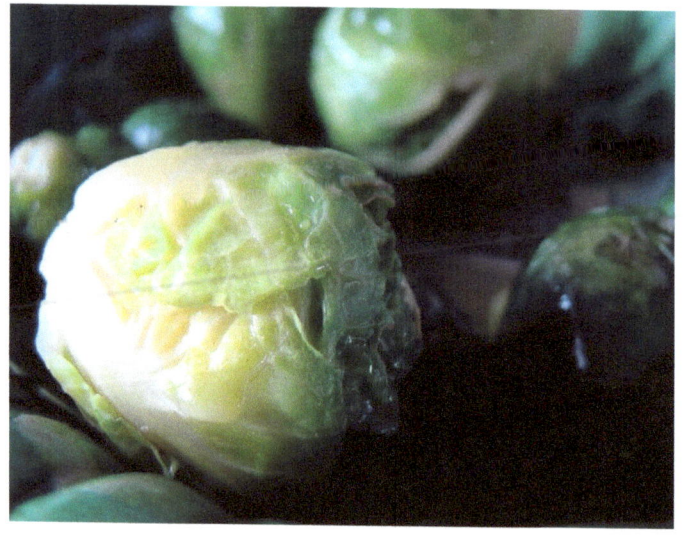

45. Just a Sprout

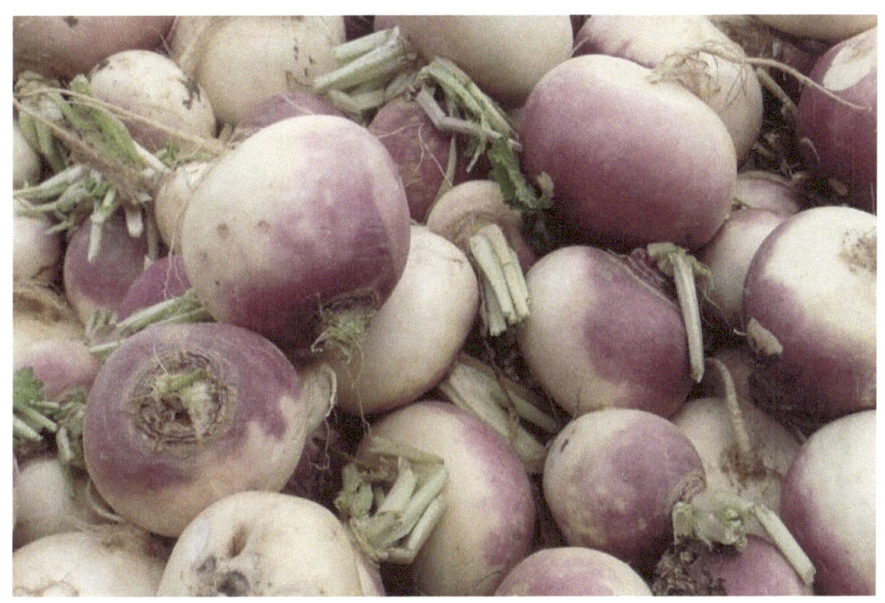

46. Invasion of the Killer Turnips

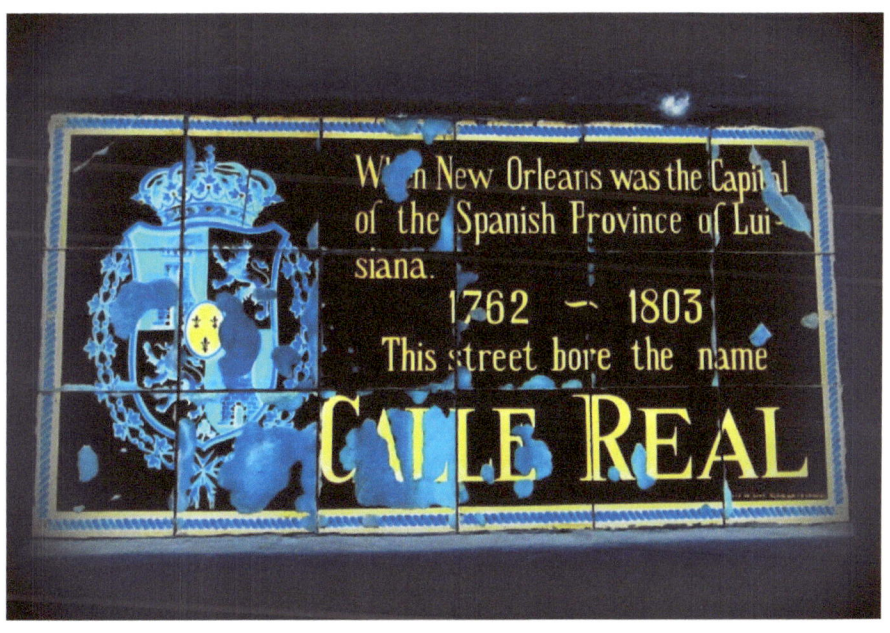

47. New Orleans – Calle Real

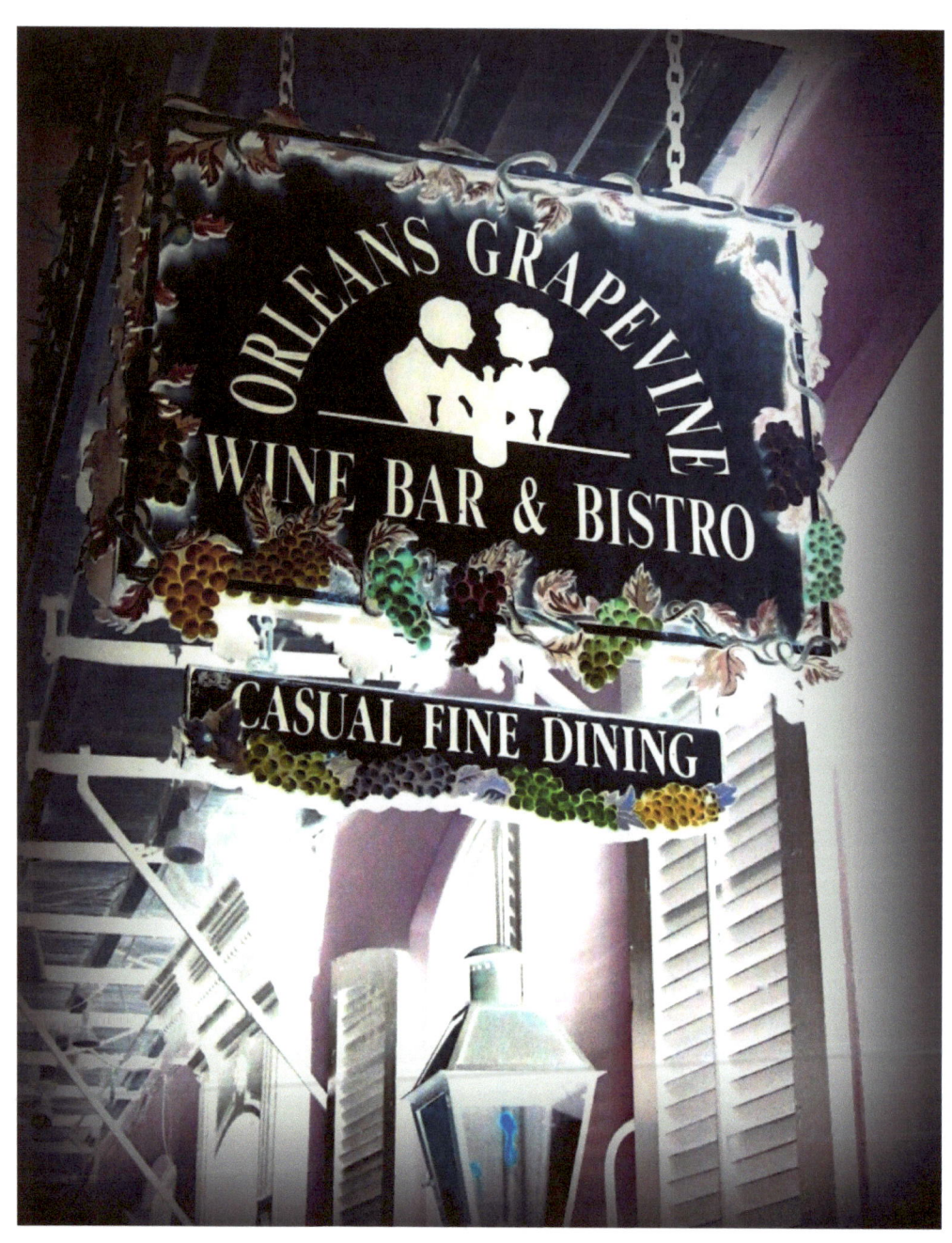

48. A Light Lunch Perhaps?

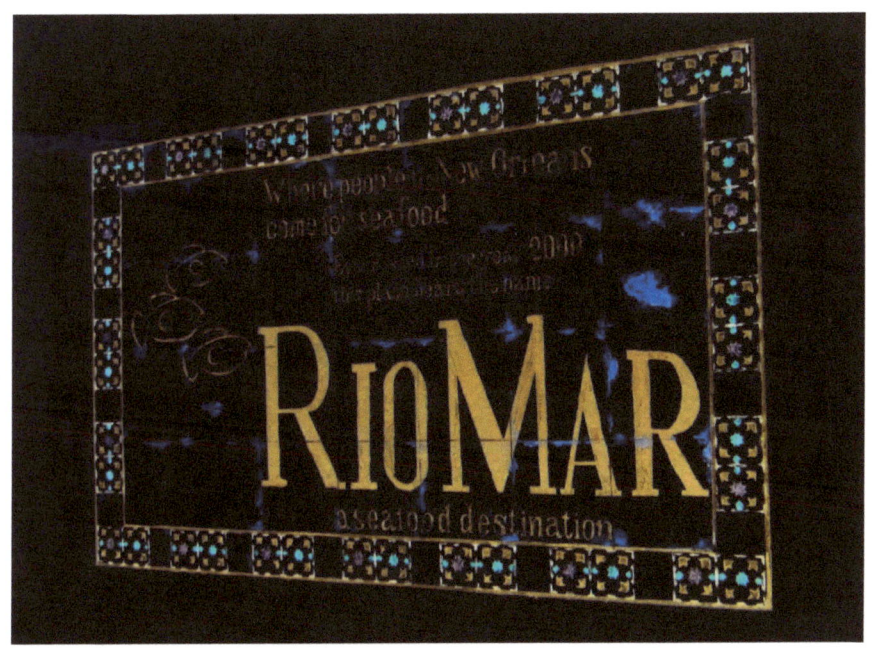

49. A Fine Seafood Destination in New Orleans

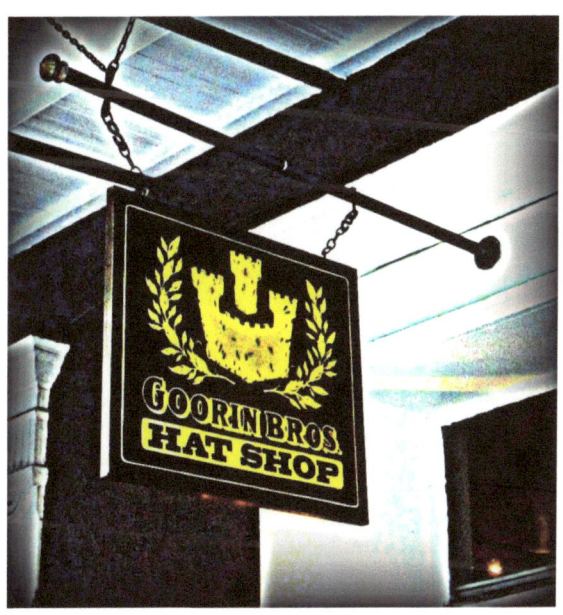

50. Capping it all off